REMOTEtional
INTELLIGENGE

Live Training Events

REMOTEtional Intelligence is part of a 5-part live training series, available though pmplicity.com. Other live training events include:

- Make it Manageable

- Transcending Team Dysfunction

- Adapt and Win!

- 30 Days Faster!

To register for the next REMOTEtional Intelligence live training event, visit **https://www.pmplicity.com/play1** or scan the QR code below.

REMOTEtional
INTELLIGENGE

How to use Emotional Intelligence
to deliver optimal performance
from any location

Jerry Reed, EQI, PMP, CSM, MCP
Yolanda Reed, CSM

Contents

Preface

For over 20 years, I worked from home as a project management professional with AT&T. During that time, I experienced 4 mergers, 8 reorgs and 9 new bosses. I survived at least 10 rounds of layoffs and was promoted 5 times. Of the 9 bosses I had throughout my 25-year career at AT&T, I only met 2 of them face to face. To excel, I had to learn to quickly win over bosses, teams and stakeholders, the majority of whom I'd never meet in person. This book comprises the lessons I've learned about how to work from home effectively, stay "plugged in" to the office, and effectively manage interactions with managers, co-workers, and customers. I began compiling my research when UCLA and Cedars Sinai Medical Center approached me about developing training for a work-from-home program. Their objective was to train managers and workers to maintain and deliver optimal performance from remote locations. I had been chronicling the information in this book throughout my career as a project management professional, UCLA instructor and business owner. Reflecting on my experiences and putting them onto paper was exhilarating! It was interesting to identify the tactics and emotional intelligence traits I used to deliver work outcomes, manage office politics, and remain competitive while working from home. With the help of my wife and co-author Yolanda, I've transcribed strategies and lessons learned over two decades into this book. We hope it will help you excel while working remotely, or from any location.

Introduction

On February 25th, 2020, Nancy Meissonier, MD, director of the CDC's National Center for Immunization and Respiratory Diseases, held a news conference addressing the spread of COVID 19, at which she stated "Ultimately, we expect we will see community spread in this country [the US]. It's not a question of **if** anymore. It's a question of **when**…" That day, I ordered Dr. Timothy Zahar's eBook, titled *Everything about face MASKS and Corona Virus (COVID 19)*[1].

I finished most of the book before arriving at Los Angeles Metro Headquarters that evening to deliver training to their project management professionals. I broached the topic of buying an N95 mask before the start of class, but there was little interest. Later that evening, I raised the topic with my wife, and she thought the idea a bit premature. Undeterred, I ordered two reusable N95 masks that evening. "I hope you're not expecting me to wear that thing.", she said. "And I sure hope you're not going to be wearing it next to me in public." Within 30 days, N95 masks were out of stock on Amazon. To this day, she still praises me for my caution. Arthur Schopenhauer said "All truth passes through three stages. First, it is ridiculed. Second, it is violently opposed. Third, it is accepted as being self-evident." At the time of this writing, much of the US (and the world) is trending toward the third stage when it comes to wearing masks. Notwithstanding, the pandemic has exposed subtler truths that will take longer to become self-evident. One such truth is the premise of this book – **remote work is not working**. Most organizations have hurdled the technological challenges of remote work, but this was the lowest hurdle. The high hurdles have gone largely unaddressed.

They include:

- Addressing remote worker readiness issues
- Teaching professionals to establish a sense of presence
- Monitoring, assessing, inspiring, delivering and being perceived as delivering optimal performance
- Closing trust gaps
- Addressing communication challenges

In this book, you'll learn strategies for working from home effectively, staying "plugged in" to the office and effectively managing your interactions with managers, direct reports, coworkers, and stakeholders. The target audience is remote workers who want to deliver optimal performance from any location, and managers of remote workers who want to inspire optimal performance and achieve the right balance between trust and accountability.

A recent study by the Families and Work Institute (FWI)[2] concluded that providing access to flexible work arrangements "is not related to the important outcomes that employers and employees care about like engagement, job satisfaction, health and wellbeing." To achieve these important outcomes, workers must believe they have the autonomy, trust and management support they need to do their best work. For example, when managers contact remote workers, do they feel supported or micro-managed? Do they believe their managers know what they're accomplishing for the business? Do they believe they will be evaluated fairly? Do managers believe they can achieve performance objectives with a dispersed workforce? It's not enough to provide the technology that enables remote work. Issues relating to readiness, presence, performance, trust, and communication must also be addressed to scale the hurdles that impede mobile workforce sustainability.

The Promise of Remote Work

Remote work can and should result in workers having more control over their schedules, more time with their families and communities, fewer office interruptions and visible productivity gains. Here are six benefits of remote work.

1. Elimination of commute stress.

2. Positive environmental impact

3. Recovered travel time

4. Reduced personal cost

5. Work continuance during emergencies

6. Wider talent pool

A recent study published by the Society of Human Resource Managers (SHRM)[3] underscores these benefits. It purports that employees are increasingly experiencing a time famine. Here are three key findings:

- 75% of employed parents (up from 66% in 1992) feel that they don't have enough time for their **children**.

- 61% of employees in relationships (up from 50% in 1992) feel that they don't have enough time for their **husbands, wives or partners**.

- 59% of employees (up from 55% in 2002) feel they don't have enough time for **themselves**.

These findings are consistent with a study[4] of American commute hours, conducted by the US Census Bureau and published in the Washington Post, which revealed that the average American spent 225 hours (5.6 work weeks!) commuting in 2018. If you're still on the fence about the promise of remote work, consider the table below, which rank-orders the factors that contribute most to greater employee engagement, job satisfaction and retention. The factors shaded in grey can reasonably be aligned with the benefits of remote work.

Top 6 Factors: Engagement, Job Satisfaction and Retention			
Rank	Engagement	Job Satisfaction	Rentention
1	Job Challenge/ Learning	Economic Security	Economic Security
2	Climate of respect	Work-Life fit	Work-Life fit
3	Autonomy	Climate of respect	Job Challenge/Learning
4	Work-Life fit	Autonomy	Supervisor Task Support
5	Economic Security	Supervisor Task Support	Autonomy
6	Supervisor Task Support	Job Challenge/Learning	

Adapted from 2008 National Study of the Changing Workforce, sponsored by the Families and Work Institute

The promises of remote work are not new promises. They are old promises, forcibly validated by the COVID-19 pandemic. If preexisting concerns about remote work were credible, then their consequences should have become apparent by now. The opposite is also true. If the promises of remote work are credible, they should likewise be apparent by now. If they are not, then more needs to be done to scale the high hurdles mentioned earlier.

Emotional Intelligence and Remote Work

Emotional Intelligence is a set of emotional and social skills that collectively establish how well we perceive and express ourselves, develop and maintain social relationships, cope with challenges, and use emotional information. Emotional intelligence has great utility in remote work situations. It can help the mobile workforce address readiness challenges with more creativity, enhance their sense of presence, drive and deliver optimal performance, close trust gaps and communicate more effectively. At the end of each chapter, we will review the relevant aspects of Emotional Intelligence, using the EQi-2.0 model and share tactics for using them to overcome remote work challenges. The EQi-2.0 Emotional Intelligence model categorizes 15 emotional intelligence traits under five composite areas, including Self-Perception, Self-Expression, Interpersonal Skills, Decision Making Skills, and Stress Management.

The following table shows the 15 emotional intelligence traits and the composite areas their categorized under.

Self-Perception	Self-Expression	Interpersonal Skills	Desicion Making Skills	Stress Management Skills
Self-Regard	Emotional Expression	Interpersonal Relationships	Problem Solving	Flexibility
Self-Actualization	Assertiveness	Empathy	Reality Testing	Stress Tolerance
Emotional Self-Awareness	Independence	Social Responsibility	Impulse Control	Optimism

In this book, we will describe how these 15 emotional intelligence traits can benefit remote workers by enhancing remote worker readiness, presence, performance, trust, and communication.

The following table shows the 15 emotional intelligence traits and the remote worker challenge areas they can best enhance.

Readiness	Presence	Performance	Trust	Communication
Problem Solving	Interpersonal Relationships	Self-Actualization	Reality Testing	Emotional Self-Awareness
Impulse Control	Empathy	Assertiveness	Flexibility	Emotional Expression
Independence	Social Responsibility	Optimism	Self-Regard	Stress Tolerance

When you're done with this book, you'll have the strategies you need to deliver and drive optimal performance from any location.

You'll be able to:

- ✓ Explain why remote work should increase performance.
- ✓ Identify your strengths and weaknesses as a remote worker.
- ✓ Implement strategies to immediately improve remote performance.
- ✓ Distinguish performance issues from remote worker readiness issues.
- ✓ Describe the tools required for optimal remote work.
- ✓ Describe effective communication strategies for working remotely.
- ✓ Describe effective ways to establish a sense of presence.
- ✓ Provide effective responses to 7 common concerns about remote work.
- ✓ Describe effective monitoring and trust strategies.
- ✓ Identify 5 objective, pandemic-proof performance measures.
- ✓ Describe effective strategies for closing trust gaps.
- ✓ Use emotional intelligence to overcome remote work challenges.

1

Readiness

Whether you call it telework, telecommuting, remote working, working virtually, distance working or simply working from home, it's important to establish a common understanding. Telework is a **routine** or **situational** flexible work arrangement where an employee performs work duties and responsibilities from an **agreed upon** remote location. The table below captures this distinction with supporting examples.

ROUTINE VS. SITUATIONAL REMOTE WORK	
ROUTINE	**SITUATIONAL**
Ongoing and regular Examples: • Daily • Up to 3 days per week • 2 arbitrary days per week • 2 agreed upon days per week	Approved on a case-by-case basis Examples: • Inclement weather • Doctor's appointment • Medical exception • Pandemic

Whether the arrangement is routine or situational, the two most important words in this definition are **agreed upon**. A common understanding is key. For example, all parties must clarify whether remote work means working from anywhere or from an agreed upon location. Does your arrangement allow you to fly to Hawaii and work from your hotel for a week? Some managers will be indifferent, as long as the work gets done. Others will not. They will consider your home office as the dedicated remote work location. No telework policy can cover every imaginable scenario. Don't presume or plan to ask for forgiveness. Err on the side of over communication. The promise of remote work can only be realized when there is a common understanding. With this as a foundation, let's begin scaling the high hurdle of remote worker readiness.

Hitting the Rewind Button

Consider the planning that would have occurred if we knew 6 months in advance the pandemic was coming and that impacted businesses must develop a fully remote work force to continue operating. How might companies have prepared for this? Every part of every business, from IT to Sales would have launched transition programs. These programs might have implemented communication protocols, equipment standards, management training on how to lead a mobile workforce, soft skills training aimed at creating environments that balance trust with accountability, and much more. They would have been an essential prerequisite for a successful mobile workforce launch, and they are still required now. If the hastily launched mobile workforce of the new normal is to be successful, the proper starting point is remote worker readiness. It's important to recognize that clearing the technology hurdle does not equate to clearing the more formidable hurdles of readiness, presence, performance, trust, and communication. In this chapter, we'll review strategies for assessing and increasing your readiness for remote work – even if you're already working remotely. We'll focus on your readiness level in terms of dependent care, household dynamics, workspace, equipment, technology and organizational and planning skills.

Assessing Your Remote Worker Readiness Level

The following assessment is designed to assess your remote worker readiness level. Answer each question on a 1–10 scale, with 1 being low and 10 being high, then total your score. The maximum score is 100.

REMOTE READINESS ASSESSMENT	
CATEGORY	**SCORE**
Comfort Level	
1. How comfortable are you working away from your manager, co-workers, and customers?	
Dependent Care	
2. How effective are your dependent care arrangements (e.g., child-care, elder care)?	
Household Dynamics	
3. How suitable are your household dynamics for remote work?	
Workspace	
4. How suitable is your remote workspace?	
Organization Skills	
5. How organized are you?	
Planning Skills	
6. How effective are your planning skills?	
Time Management Skills	
7. How effective are your time management skills?	
Equipment	
8. How suitable is your equipment for remote work? (lighting, green screen, webcam, mic, internet speed)	
Technical Comfort Level	
9. How comfortable are you with remote work technology? (webcam, modem, VPN, Virtual Desktops)	
Communication	
10. How effective are your communications with your manager, coworkers, and customers?	

Increasing Your Remote Worker Readiness Level

To increase your remote worker readiness level, you'll need to effectively address each of the following:

- Dependent Care Readiness (E.g., Childcare, Elder Care)

- Household Readiness

- Workspace Readiness

- Equipment Readiness

- Technological Readiness

- Organizational and Planning Skill Readiness

Unaddressed challenges in any these areas can easily be misinterpreted as performance issues. For example, a dependent care issue can pull you away from your desk, resulting in your presence indicator appearing idle for an extended amount of time. A dysfunctional household dynamic can cause you to mute your phone and shut off your camera, giving others the impression that you're not engaged during meetings. An improper workspace setup can make you appear less professional than you really are. These can include poor lighting, a cluttered background or simply struggling to get your devices to work properly. Finally, poor time-management and organizational skills, can make you to appear unreliable in a remote environment. Each of these areas are poor performance imposters that can detract from your professional image. Let's present you in your best light (pun intended) by tackling them one at a time.

Dependent Care Solutions

Of all the poor performance imposters, dependent care issues are the most challenging. They put you in the difficult position of having to choose between caring for your job and a child or other dependent. Many professionals choose to save money and try to balance remote work with dependent care. They assume that the two can be merged effectively, and that in the "new normal", everyone gets a pass on dependent care disruptions. Does such a pass really exist? If so, how long can the disruption last before it becomes unprofessional? Could some managers view such disruptions as hinderances to your productivity? These are questions every professional should ponder. The truth is both work and dependent care are important enough to warrant 100% focus. Traditionally, they have never mixed well. The key to dependent care readiness is to effectively compartmentalize the two. To minimize disruptions, consider designating a dependent care provider during work hours. If your budget is limited, consider paying a member of your family or household. Also, consider collaborating with your employer to find creative ways to address your dependent care issues. Remote work is a collaborative agreement between employer and employee. The employer is entrusting the employee to deliver the same performance they would in an office environment. The employee is sharing their home to ensure there is no work stoppage. Both parties have a vested interest in a successful dependent care arrangement.

Household Drama Solutions

Not all home dynamics are ideal for remote work. Some professionals would never choose to blend their household and work dynamics. There may be significant challenges at home that prevent working from home effectively. The spillover of household dysfunction into professional life is a consequence of the two being forcibly merged. Household dysfunction can include abusive family members, volatile relationships, and household members with substance abuse or mental health issues. These household dynamics can cause even the most capable professionals to feel helpless. Household dysfunction can be emotionally draining and make you appear inattentive and unenergetic. It's difficult to bring your best self to work when you're emotionally depleted by mid-day. If these words are resonating with you, you're not alone. According to a Pew survey[5], 46% of Americans have a family member or friend with a current or past drug addiction. Also, about 1 in 4 adults suffer from a diagnosable mental health disorder each year. To work effectively from home, you'll need to find ways to preserve enough of your energy and emotions to deliver effective work outcomes. Here are eight tactics you can apply right now.

1. **Prepare yourself.** Proactively identify root causes and emotional triggers and take time to prepare yourself for the challenges ahead. Get up early enough to center yourself with a walk, a workout, or a warm bath. Think about how to prevent or minimize negative encounters ahead of time. Also, work with a professional to develop proactive coping strategies.

2. **Control what you can.** You may not be able to control someone's reactions or behaviors, but with practice and good counsel, you can learn to control your responses. The better you can control your responses, the less oxygen you'll provide for emotional flareups.

3. **Talk it through.** Sometimes you'll need to deal with the matter head on. In these cases, study proven tactics for navigating difficult conversations. The best-selling book "Crucial Conversations" is an excellent place to start. It'll teach you to balance the content of the conversation with the safety conditions required for effectively navigating emotional talks.

4. **Set an emotional abuse limit.** To do this effectively, you'll need to monitor yourself. Pay attention to biological changes like rising heart rate, changes in your rate of speech or sweating to determine when your emotional limit is approaching. When it's close, find a graceful way to exit the encounter. The key is to step away when your limit is approaching and not after it has been surpassed. Be mindful that you may take some emotional shots during your graceful exit. Take them gracefully and don't return fire. Take a short walk if you need to before resuming your work.

5. **Replenish yourself.** Don't let yesterday's emotions carry over to today. One of the best ways to do this is to take a physical or mental break – a run, a workout, a bike ride, a good show, a swim, or long walk can work wonders.

6. **Set reasonable expectations.** You know your household. Don't expect immediate results because you've armed yourself with new tactics. Even proven tactics need time to work. Effective tactics can be easy to learn, but difficult to master. Be patient with yourself and your household.

7. **Bring in the Experts.** If you're not getting the results you want, take a page from the NBA and get more talent. Seek professional help. One of the most underutilized resources available to professionals today is Employee Assistance Programs (EAPs). Here's a list of services offered by most EAPs.

   - Child Care

   - Elder Care

   - Financial Consultation

   - Legal Consultation

   - Counseling

- Life Coaching

- Identity Theft

8. **Negotiate a remote location.** Many professionals are reluctant to inform their manager of work-life balance issues. In some cases, this is wise. However, if dysfunctional household dynamics get mistaken for performance issues the outcome can be worse. If all else fails, consider engaging your manager with a solution-oriented approach. You may be able to negotiate working from someplace other than your house. Perhaps that remote location can be the office.

Workspace Solutions

Many professionals work in suboptimal workspaces due to the limitations of their square footage or the lack of a dedicated room for a home office. Suboptimal workspaces can adversely affect your performance and professional image. While there may be restrictions on space, there is no restriction on creativity and level of effort. You can create an efficient workspace and maintain your professional image irrespective of your space constraints. Remember, it's not your entire home that needs a makeover; only the 65% viewing range of your webcam. This is done in Hollywood every day. Also, you don't need a dedicated room for an office, just an ergonomic seating and desk arrangement. Consider the following image. Why is this workspace unsuitable? Is it limited space or limited creativity and effort? This workspace clearly suffers from the latter.

Unsuitable
Remote
workspace

- Minimal Creativity
- Low Level of Effort
- Low Household Collaboration

Now consider the next image. It has similar same space constraints. The clear improvements are the result of increased creativity and effort.

Suitable
Remote
workspace

- High Creativity
- High Level of Effort
- High Household Collaboration

Creativity

The first step toward improving workspace readiness is to get creative. Following are four inspiring examples of professionals who used creativity to overcome constraints. They may not all meet the eight ideal workspace requirements we'll discuss in the next section, but they can trigger your own creativity and get you started on the right path.

Example 1 — Household Constraints

- Karen and her husband Kevin live in a small Manhattan apartment.

- They have a young child.

- They're both attorneys working from home.

- They have only one desk with a monitor, which Karen uses.

- Kevin's work requires a quiet environment.

- There are no spare rooms in the apartment

Example 1 — Creative Solution — "The Bathtub Desk"

Kevin created the quiet workspace he needed by placing a chair and a small ironing board in their bathtub. While this is not the most ergonomic set up, it's certainly a creative solution.

Example 2 — Household Constraints

- Sheila is a keynote speaker.

- Her in-person events were canceled or moved online.

- She has small children.

- Quiet is a must.

- The most meeting-friendly background is her bedroom.

- Her bedroom has no extra space.

Example 2 — Creative Solution - "The Ladder Desk"

Sheila used a ladder as a "podium" to deliver her speaking engagements in a quiet environment.

Example 3 — Household Constraints

- Jesse works in strategy for a software company.

- He shares a small San Francisco condo with his wife.

- They both work from home.

- They're both in meetings all day.

- There's no noise barrier.

Example 3 —Creative Solution - "The SUV Desk"

Jesse used a piece of wood for a desk to set up a private office in his SUV.

Example 4 — Constraints

- Zoe lives in Fort Wayne, Indiana.

- She works for a commercial insurance company .

- Her kitchen and living room are unavailable.

- She's operating from her cluttered basement.

- She uses three monitors.

Creative Solution - "The Ping Pong Office"

Zoe gets high marks for creativity! She created a desk and and office using a ping-pong table.

Effort (Creating an Ideal Workspace)

Now that your creative juices are flowing, you'll need a set of ideals to focus your efforts. Following are eight criteria for an ideal workspace.

1. **Silence.** Collaborate with your household to create the silence you need to deliver effective work outcomes. Avoid working in high-traffic areas where it would be unreasonable to expect a low noise level.

2. **Solitude.** Officemates differ from housemates, in that everyone is focused on work (or should be!). If you're working next to someone who is playing a video game, watching a movie, or engaged in a heated debate, it's difficult to focus. To do your best work, you must create an isolated environment for peak concentration. The SUV and bathtub desks shown above are creative ways to create solitude.

3. **Clutter-free.** A cluttered space contributes to a cluttered mind. It's important to create and maintain a clutter-free workspace throughout the day. Dedicate a space that's reserved for your work and deem it off limits for storing other household items until after work hours.

4. **Distraction-free.** One of the benefits of remote work is freedom from office interruptions. Don't swap one distraction for another. Social media alerts or sensationalized "breaking news" are very effective at capturing and holding your attention. Consider silencing your smart phone notifications during selective work hours or investing in apps created for that purpose.

5. **Room temperature.** The temperature of your environment can affect your performance at work. According to a study[6] conducted by Lawrence Berkey Lab, an ideal room temperature can extend your hours of productivity. The results show that performance increases with temperature up to 69°F (21°C) and decreases with temperature above 73°F (23°C). The highest productivity was at 71°F (22°C). Further, at 83°F (30°C), there was an 8.9% productivity drop from the maximum productivity observed at 71°F (22°C).

6. **Good lighting.** Along with an ideal room temperature, good lighting is the silent partner of productive work outcomes. It mitigates tiredness and increases concentration level. A good mix of daylight and artificial light is recommended. The ideal room illuminance for computer work is 500 lux. This number increases with age and with the complexity of the task. According to lightingdeluxe.com, productivity gains can be realized as lighting is increased from 500 lux to 1000 lux. To put this into context, hospital lighting is typically 1000 lux, supermarkets are typically 750 lux and showrooms are typically 500 lux. As we'll see in the next section, good lighting is also important for presenting a professional image on camera.

7. **Comfortable chair.** Did you know that office chairs are categorized by the number of hours you can work comfortably in them? If you want to deliver 8 hours of productivity, you'll need to invest in an 8-hour chair. Equipment recommendations are included in the next section.

8. **Ample desk space.** Desk size and shape can change posture, comfort, and productivity. The depth of your desk (measured by stretching your arms forward) should be between 20 and 30 inches. The width (measured by stretching your arms side to side) should be at least 24 inches. If you're between 5 feet and 6 ½ feet tall, your desk height should be between 28 and 30 inches.

Equipment Solutions

As the saying goes, "a worker is only as good as their tools". Having the right equipment is essential for maintaining a professional image while working from home. The following equipment list is what we use in our home office. It's not a budget-friendly list. It's an investment that will yield handsome returns in your work productivity and professional image. This list is not meant to endorse one product over another. We recommend using it to benchmark the grade of equipment you should consider for presenting a professional image and achieving effective work outcomes.

1. **Noise Cancellation Headphones.** Sometimes you won't be able to control the noise level or achieve the solitude you need to deliver quality work. A good set of noise cancellation headphones can produce the quiet and sense of solitude you need to be effective. We use the Bose NC 700 (NC stands for Noise Cancellation) headphones. It has three noise cancellation settings. The maximum noise cancellation level (10) is quite effective.

Recommend Bose NC700s

2. **Office Chair (8-hours).** As mentioned earlier, office chairs are categorized by the number of hours they will deliver comfort throughout the workday. At a minimum, you'll want to invest in an 8-hour chair. We use the 8-hour executive chair by La-Z-Boy.

Recommend Ergonomic + 8-hour rating
E.g. LazyBoy

3. **Quality Webcam.** In the new normal, investing in a sharper image goes well beyond clothing. If your likeness is not sharp on the screen, it can detract from your professional image. The world has come to expect 1080p at a minimum and most built-in webcams deliver 720p. We alternate between the Logitech c920 and the Logitech Brio. Both render 1080p images and the Brio renders up to 4K.

Recommend Logitech Brio

4. **Quality Lighting.** Photographer Trent Parke said, "Light turns the ordinary into the magical". Of all the recommended equipment, quality lighting will make the greatest visible difference in your professional image. A $60.00 investment can make you outshine (literally) your colleagues. Conversely, poor lighting can diminish your professional appearance. We use a Yesker 18 Inch 65W LED ring light kit with tripod stand.

Recommend Yesker 18 Inch 65W LED ring light kit

5. **Fast Internet Speed.** Ironically, internet speed is often overlooked in the context of remote work. Chances are your criteria for selecting a carrier are different today than when you signed your contract. A slow connection can erode hard-won enhancements to your professional image. Depending on your number of streaming devices, it may be in your best interest to upgrade your plan or select the fastest carrier in your area. You may be surprised how much faster your connection can be for a similar price point.

Recommend fastest provider in your area

6. **Signal Booster.** Even if you have a fast internet connection, the further your home office is from your router, the less potent your signal. A signal booster can increase your signal to remote parts of your home. Before making such an investment, check with your carrier to confirm compatibility with your router.

Contact your internet provider!

Technological Solutions

Use the following table to assess and improve your technological readiness across ten key areas.

	Technological Area	Improvement Consideration
1	Cyber Security	• Cyber Security training • Password apps • Shredder
2	Connectivity	• Investigate carriers • Signal booster • Ethernet cable
3	Technical Support	• Company Help Desk • Vendor Support • Third Party Support
4	Equipment Acquisition	• Company-issued equipment • Company discounts • Company P-card allowances
5	Equipment Installation	• Company Help Desk • Vendor Installation • Third Party Installation

	Technological Area	Improvement Consideration
6	Equipment Maintenance and Repair	• Company Help Desk • Vendor Maintenance • Third Party Maintenance
7	Software requirements and Standards	• Company policy/standards • Vendor policy/standards • Online support manuals
8	Remote access procedures	• Company policy/standards • Company training • speedtest.net
9	Data Storage and Backup	• Company policy/standards • Cloud providers • Local Storage Devices
10	Compatibility with Office Technology	• Company policy/standards • Company training

Organizational and Planning Solutions

Remote work makes some weaknesses more apparent, including poor communication, social, planning, and organizational skills. Working in an office environment can mask these weaknesses because there are more opportunities to cover them in real time. For example, if you hear coworkers discussing an important announcement at the microwave, you can ask one of them to forward you a copy—even though you both know there's already a copy in your inbox. A candid assessment of the following areas will help you develop action plans to increase your organizational readiness for effective remote work.

Disorganized Inbox

A disorganized inbox means you're not current. It can make you appear distracted and unfocussed on work events. An office environment can mask this weakness because others can keep you informed more readily.

Here are two simple things you can do to turn this weakness into a strength.

1. **Delay filing emails.** It takes one minute to read an email and up to five minutes to file it. By reading and deleting emails, you can read 60 emails per hour instead of 12. If you come across emails that truly need to be filed, flag it, and move to the next message. **Do not** make another folder for this purpose. Keep it simple. Read and delete or flag and move on.

2. **Organize your inbox.** Effective folder structures go a long way in managing office communications. If organization is not your strong suit, seek guidance from a colleague that has an organized inbox. You'll recognize them because they're always in the know on late-breaking communications. Ask them to take a screenshot of their folder structure and send it to you. They'll probably be flattered that you took notice.

Low Daily Task Completion Percentage

Daily throughput is important for remote workers because it is an objective measure of productivity. Some managers will be checking for productivity declines resulting from the transition to remote work. Therefore, it's in your best interest to increase your daily task completion percentage. If you generally complete less than 50% of your daily or weekly task list, or if you don't create a task list at all, this section will prove helpful. It includes simple things you can do to increase your daily throughput.

1. **Make a <u>complete</u> task list**. To increase your task completion percentage, you must first know what those tasks are. Making a daily or weekly task list forces you to take a wholistic view of your workload. It's a brainstorming exercise to capture 100% of the tasks you've committed to completing and 100% of the tasks required to complete that week's deliverables. It's the best way to ensure you don't lose track of important action items.

2. **Prioritize your task list.** Most of us have more tasks than can be completed in a workday. Therefore, we must identify and focus on the most important tasks. Prioritizing your task list can help increase the value of your work outcomes by focusing your efforts toward accomplishing the most important deliverables. It also focuses your efforts toward fully completing targeted deliverables, rather than partially completing random tasks. We'll discuss task prioritization in greater detail in an upcoming section.

3. **Set a lower daily task limit.** The Kanban agile approach sets a Work in Progress (WIP) limit because we can only discover our true productivity rate by measuring it in real time. Discover your true productivity rate by setting your daily task limit in small, achievable increments. If your goal is to complete 80% — 100% of your task list per day, use trial and error to set realistic goals. For example, don't set a goal to clear your entire inbox. Set a goal to read

and delete 25 messages. Think of it like lifting weights. Start with what you can comfortably handle and increase it over time as your strength (efficiency) grows.

Missed Deadlines

Several things contribute to missed deadlines, including poor planning, ineffective project management and simply having more work than you can handle. One of the most subtle contributors is poor prioritization. If everything on your task list is an **A** priority, then nothing is an **A** priority. Your system for prioritizing tasks must include clear criteria for **A** vs **B** vs **C** priority tasks. One of the best ways to avoid missing important deadlines is to prioritize tasks with important deadlines as **A** priority tasks. Because these tasks often take up the whole day or week, they get prioritized below tasks with shorter durations. This is a common practice. We often postpone time-consuming tasks and underestimate the time required to complete them. This can be problematic because oftentimes you can only know how much time a task will take by working on it. By starting it early, you'll have plenty of time to discover its true time requirement and collaborate with your manager and stakeholders to offload less important work. The point is, when you make your task list, don't prioritize by efficiency or preference. Use objective criteria to decide what to work on first. Does the task have a deadline? Is your manager concerned about when this task will get done? Have you committed to completing this task by a certain date? These are good reasons to make a task an **A** priority. You'll know you're doing it right if you often find yourself working on tasks that you're the least excited to work on or if you start working on tasks earlier than you think you should. Stick with this approach and you'll get much better at making deadlines.

Poor Time Management

When you're working in the office, it's usually not a big deal if you get back from lunch 15 minutes later than you said you would – especially if you were out with co-workers. Contrast that with working from home and leaving a message on your presence indicator that you'll be "Back at 1PM". When you arrive at your desk at 1:15PM, you'll probably have an instant message waiting for you. This won't ruin your professional image, but it can tarnish it a little, especially if the message was left by your boss. Poor time management has less forgiveness in remote work situations because interactions are more contractual in nature. Written postings incline readers to interpret them literally. You may be tempted not to publish specific return times to get a bit of wiggle room, but you'll be missing out on a great opportunity to establish presence and earn trust, which we'll discuss in later chapters. It's best to sharpen your time management skills.

Here are some tips to help you do that.

1. **Check your calendar when you start working.** Newsflash – being late to a meeting because the meeting organizer didn't include a reminder is your fault, not theirs. Know your calendar. Not only will you be aware of your scheduled events, you'll also know how much prep time you have between them. Consider printing your daily Outlook agenda. Out of sight, out of mind.

2. **Just say no.** It's tempting to underestimate the time requirements when you really want to do something. For example, I feel entitled to a hot Soy Chai Tea Latte every time I teach a course. But even though my coffee shop is just up the road, it takes 15 minutes to get to the drive-through, 15 minutes to wait in line, 15 minutes to drive back and 15 minutes to get back into my workflow. Therefore, unless I set aside an hour for it (which I usually can't justify), it's best for me to say no.

3. **Choose 45 minutes early over 15 minutes late.** For reasons I cannot explain, there's always the option of being 45 minutes early to an event or 15 minutes late. Busy professionals cannot fathom wasting 45 minutes, so we'd rather chance being late. Sometimes, we can manage to beat the buzzer, but the cost is being out of breath and uncomposed. The better choice is to choose to be 45 minutes early. You can use the time to complete a task on your list or practice looking smug when a colleague arrives late.

4. **Watch the clock.** Even though the time is on our computers, phones, and smart watches, we still manage to lose track of time. Put a big digital clock in your direct field of vision and it'll work wonders!

5. **Check tomorrow's calendar before you stop working.** Do this without fail. Sometimes you'll find last-minute meetings in different time zones, meetings you forgot were on the calendar or meetings for which you'll want to stay late or start early to prepare.

Emotional Intelligence and Readiness

The emotional intelligence skills that can have the greatest impact on remote worker readiness are Problem Solving, Impulse Control and Independence. Following are definitions of each emotional intelligence skill, indicators of high and low effectiveness and steps you can take to improve.

Problem Solving

Remote work presents a host of new problems to solve, including troubleshooting technical issues, addressing relationship challenges at home, solving dependent care issues, and developing an ideal work-from-home setup. From an emotional intelligence standpoint, **problem solving** is the ability to find solutions to problems in situations where emotions are involved. It includes the ability to understand how emotions impact decision making. The following table includes indicators of high and low effectiveness using this emotional intelligence trait.

Low Effectiveness	High Effectiveness
• Jumps into solution • Flies by seat of pants • Uses unstructured strategy	• Gathers information first, and weighs pros and cons • Can identify and solve problems • Uses a systematic problem-solving approach

Here's a 6-step approach you can use to be more systematic in how you solve problems.

1. Examine the problem.

2. Generate alternatives.

3. Evaluate each alternative.

4. Select the best alternative.

5. Implement the best alternative.

6. Assess the outcome.

Impulse Control

As mentioned earlier, it's difficult to bring your best self to work when you're emotionally depleted due to an emotional encounter with a member of your household or family. Also, when processing work-related communications, messages can appear more aggressive or condescending than the sender intends. It's important to have the ability to delay emotional responses until all the facts are known. From an emotional intelligence standpoint, **impulse control** is the ability to resist or delay an impulse, drive or temptation to act. It involves avoiding rash, reactionary behaviors. The following table includes indicators of high and low effectiveness using this emotional intelligence trait.

Low Effectiveness	High Effectiveness
• Explosive and unpredictable • Easily frustrated • Abusive	• Composed • High tolerance for frustration • Ability to postpone reactions

One of the strongest tactics you can use to get better at impulse control is Dr. Albert Ellis' ABCDE system[7]. Ellis is internationally recognized as the Father of Rational Emotive Behavior Theory and Therapy. His system posits that you can modify and change your feelings by using logic and deductive reasoning. Impulsive reactions are generated by the way we interpret events and not by the events themselves. Therefore, by delaying or challenging the interpretation of the event you can delay or challenge an impulsive reaction.

Here's a graphical depiction of the ABCDE model.

ABCDE Model

A – **A**ctivating event or Adversity

C – the emotinal **C**onsequences

B – **B**eliefs about Events or adversity

E – **E**ffect or consequent of challenging self defeating belief

D – **D**isputations to challenge self defeating belief

Independence

Remote work can put some emotional intelligence growth areas on full display. Independence is at the top of this list. It includes the ability to be self-directed in structuring your workday and delivering work outcomes. Some will relish this level of autonomy and others will long for the structure and support that the office provided. From an emotional intelligence standpoint, **independence** is the ability to be self-directed and free from emotional dependence upon others. It involves the ability to autonomously make decisions, plan work and complete tasks. The following table includes indicators of high and low effectiveness using this emotional intelligence trait.

Low Effectiveness	High Effectiveness
• Uncertain of own ideas	• Self-directed
• Needs protection or support	• Self-driven
• Prefers others to make final decisions	• Decisive

To become more independent, consider some of the root causes of over-reliance on others. These include the fear of failure and fear of disappointing others.

Here are tactics for overcoming each root cause.

1. **Overcome Fear of Failure.** To overcome the fear of failure, begin by considering that the consequences of failure are almost never as bad as you think they are. In most cases, the worst that will happen is you will get coaching on how to make a better decision next time. This will ultimately make you more independent by increasing your confidence in your ability to make the right choices. When we overestimate the consequences of failure, we over rely on others to make decisions or try to protect ourselves by getting others to participate in making the decision. That way, when things go wrong, we can share the blame with the group. This approach decreases self-confidence and your ability to make fresh contributions to the business. I'm reminded of chess players who learn the game by memorizing sequences rather than experimenting with new tactics. Such players can always be beaten by trading a few pieces with them and forcing them to be original.

2. **Overcome Fear of Disappointing Others.** We all want to be liked and accepted. Some take this too far and avoid making decisions that will disappoint the crowd. They hedge their bets by getting as many reactions as possible before making a decision and then making the most popular choice. This approach can be effective in overly political environments. Sometimes it's in your best interest to refrain from "making waves". Taken too far though, this approach can make you invisible. Others will soon pick up on this tendency and stop looking to you for original ideas. They will only consult you when they need support for their original ideas. In other words, to overcome the fear of disappointing others, consider the consequences. You may be trading in your originality for popularity. In the words of Herman Melville, "It is better to fail in originality than to succeed in imitation."

Chapter Summary

In this chapter, we defined remote work and discussed the benefits it promises. We reviewed strategies for assessing and increasing remote worker readiness levels in terms of dependent care, household, workspace, equipment, technology, and organizational and planning skills. We concluded with strategies for increasing emotional intelligence in the areas of Problem Solving, Impulse Control and Independence. For additional tactics, see **Appendix A** which includes effective responses to seven common concerns about working from home. The COVID 19 pandemic has caused many business leaders to rethink the notion of a headquarters location, and the need to have employees perform their work from one company location each day of the week. As this trend continues, it will be increasingly important to identify and close remote worker readiness gaps.

References

1. Zahar, Timothy. Everything about face MASKS and Corona Virus (COVID 19). Dr. Timothy Zahar, 2020.

2. Families and Work Institute. 2008 National Study of the Changing Workforce (NSCW). FWI, 2008.

3. Society of Human Resource Managers (SHRM). "Flexibility: Central to an Effective Workplace" shrm.org, Ellen Galinsky, 09/01/16, https://www.shrm.org/hr-today/trends-and-forecasting/special-reports-and-expert-views/pages/ellen-galinsky.aspx.

4. Washington Post US/Census Bureau. "Nine days on the Road. Average commute time reached a record last year." washingtonpost.com, Christopher Ingraham, 10/07/19, https://www.washingtonpost.com/business/2019/10/07/nine-days-road-average-commute-time-reached-new-record-last-year/.

5. Pew Research Center. "Nearly half of Americans have a family member or close friend who's been addicted to drugs". pewresearch.org, John Gramlich, 10/26/17, https://www.pewresearch.org/fact-tank/2017/10/26/nearly-half-of-americans-have-a-family-member-or-close-friend-whos-been-addicted-to-drugs/.

6. Lawrence Berkeley Lab. "Effect of Temperature on Office Environment". Indoor. lbl.gov, Olli Seppanen, William J. Fisk and QH Lei, July, 2006, https://indoor.lbl.gov/sites/all/files/lbnl-60946.pdf.

7. Ellis, Albert. Feeling Better, Getting Better, Staying Better. Impact Publishers, 2001.

2

Presence

The ability to project a sense of **presence** is essential for remote work. Presence is the quality of being unseen, but present. It's the ability to project to others the sense that you're with them when you're not. It's the confidence they have that you can be reached when they need you. Think of one of your closest confidants. They can be hundreds of miles away, but you feel like they're available and accessible whenever you need them. If you can't reach them, you know there's a good reason and that they'll get back to you at their earliest opportunity. That's what presence is. It's having the right mix of **availability** (able to be used), **accessibility** (able to be reached) and **affinity** (able to be felt). To increase your sense of presence, you'll need to amplify the sense that you're able to be used, reached, and felt.

Amplifying Availability

Your availability (ability to be used) is not determined solely by you. It's also not determined by whether you or your manager think you can take on extra work. In a well-run organization, availability is determined by business priority. These priorities should be set by leadership and disseminated to the workforce through S.M.A.R.T. goals. These goals should be referenced whenever there is new work or a shift in priority. They shouldn't be used as a basis for rejecting new work, but as a reference point to ensure the work remains aligned with business priority. Here are some things you can do to amplify your sense of availability to your manager, co-workers, and stakeholders.

1. **Broadcast what you're working on.** As communications migrate from e-mail to instant messaging, your presence indicator takes on more significance. If your presence indicator simply reads "Available", you're wasting an opportunity to amplify your contributions to the business. Consider posting a message that broadcasts what you're working on, E.g., "Updating Timelines" or "Generating Reports". Also, when you broadcast what you're working on, start with a verb. Instead of broadcasting "Project Meeting", broadcast "Hosting a Project Meeting". It emphasizes the actions you're taking to move the business forward. If you're not hosting the meeting, post something like "Planning Meeting", which implies action.

2. **Get others to broadcast what you're working on.** Nothing builds presence with your manager better than when co-workers and colleagues tell them what you're working on. It sends a message that you're collaborating with others and getting things done. The best way to do this is to simply ask. Here are two examples:

   - *"Would you mind including my manager when you send your next update?"*

   - *"Can you ask our manager how we should handle this, since your 1-on-1 meeting is before mine this week?"*

3. **Reconfirm Priorities.** Look for opportunities to reconfirm your work priorities with your manager. This will not only confirm you're working on the right things but also keep them current on your availability or lack thereof. Ironically, one of the best indicators that you've established presence with your manager is when they know that you're **not** available and must focus on a key initiative. Don't assume they're always aware of what you're working on. Check in occasionally and reconfirm you're prioritizing the right work.

4. **Don't "Sandbag".** Don't give in to the temptation to delay closing out projects as a means of managing your workload. Managers have a broad field of vision. They know what everyone's working on and can quickly rattle off who's truly overloaded and who's "sandbagging". If you sandbag in the card game of Spades, the penalty is generally 9 points. If you do it at work, the penalty is

much greater. You could lose credibility with your manager. Credibility loss is especially damaging in remote work situations, where trust is already fragile.

5. **Get available.** The best way to amplify your availability is to do just that. Find ways to close projects faster so you can be available to take on more work. In the post-COVID business environment, efficient workers will be among the few groups in demand. For insights on how to close projects faster, consider taking the 2-hour live course "30 Days Faster!", offered at pmplicity.com.

Amplifying Accessibility

Your accessibility (ability to be reached) is as much about perception as it is reality. While it's important your manager can reach you when they need to, the fact is, they will rarely need to. It's more important that they <u>think</u> they can reach you. They may only try to reach you 5% of the time. The other 95% of the time, they will either think they <u>can</u> reach you if they need to, or they <u>cannot</u>. What they think will be largely determined by how well you amplify your sense of accessibility. Here are some things you can do to enhance this important aspect of presence.

1. **Broadcast how to reach you.** You can let your manager and stakeholders know that they can reach you by including a contact number on your presence indicator, that not only broadcasts what you're working on but also how they can reach you. Here's an example of a presence indicator message that works well.

   • *Updating Timelines (312-555-000, if Urgent)*

2. **Broadcast when you'll be back.** This is your opportunity to put your time management skills on display. Leaving a message that simply says "Away" can erode your sense of presence. This is because no one knows when you'll be back or how long you've been "away". Here are three simple rules to amplify your accessibility. 1. Always post a return time. 2. Always get back earlier than your posted return time. 3. Rarely respond to messages before your posted return time. The point of rule number 3 is to reinforce that your breaks are well-earned and that you intend to take them. If you're balancing dependent care with work, you'll need all the breaks you can get!

Here's an example of a presence indicator message that works well.

- *Lunch – Back at 1:00 PM, PST (312-555-000, if Urgent)*

3. **Broadcast slow response times.** If you're working on something that requires dedicated focus, let your manager, co-workers and stakeholders know your responses may be delayed. This works well when you inform them in advance. It's also a good way to carve out time to complete recurring tasks without interruption. For example, every Friday morning you might inform your manager and stakeholders that you'll be slow responding to instant messages until the afternoon because you're updating a weekly report. Here an example of a presence indicator that works well.

- *Updating Reports (Delayed Response until Noon, PST)*

4. **Broadcast relatable breaks.** This suggestion is subject to the culture at your company. Generally, there is universal empathy for the need for coffee. If coffee is a part of your company culture, you can take a much-needed coffee break without losing presence with the following presence indicator.

- *Coffee Break – Back at 3:00 PM, PST (312-555-0000, if Urgent)*

5. **Get others to broadcast when your internet is down.** If your internet is down and you're unable to work, you must have a way to contact your manager and co-workers. Otherwise, you'll run the risk of people forming their own conclusions about your absence. Even when you have justifiable technical issues, you must maintain a sense of presence. You can do this by adding the phone numbers of your manager and a few co-workers to your contact list. When you experience an outage, contact them at the start of your workday and ask them to send out a message on your behalf. Include an estimated time service will be restored. If no estimated time is available, have your colleague indicate that as well. Also, be sure to have them include your contact number.

Amplifying Affinity

Amplifying availability and accessibility can help close distance in time and space. Emotional distance is another matter entirely. To close emotional distance, you must amplify **affinity**. Affinity is a spontaneous or natural liking for someone. Once you establish it, you will have cut your work in half when it comes to establishing presence. When you have affinity with a co-worker or manager, it's easier for them to feel your presence and they're quicker to extend the benefit of the doubt when issues arise. Affinity is not always easy to establish, but here are some suggestions.

1. **Find a meaningful common interest.** There are certain interests that establish immediate rapport. For example, distance runners have a special affinity for cars bearing 13.1 or 26.2 stickers. This sort of meaningful interest can create instant affinity. Be on the lookout for meaningful common interests with your boss and key stakeholders.

2. **Ask genuinely about someone's day, family, or hobby.** The operative word is genuine. Everyone asks how you're doing but few really want to know. This is especially helpful with managers, because most professionals are so busy complaining to them that they rarely ask about their manager's welfare. Managers may not be inclined to divulge everything that's on their mind, but they'll appreciate that you took a genuine interest in their person.

3. **Collaborate more.** Look for ways to partner on projects and initiatives. There are simple, fun, and productive ways to do this. Have you always wanted to build a website? Partner with a like-minded colleague and submit a proposal to enhance your team's website or SharePoint page. Have you always wanted to master an app that your team uses? Partner with a different colleague and propose to develop a training session for the team about little-known tips. Is your boss always getting on the team about submitting their weekly reports? Partner with your boss and a colleague and propose a standard template to make it easier for the team to comply. Collaborating on projects together is one of the easiest ways to build alliances and amplify affinity.

Amplifying Leadership Presence

No presence is as important as leadership presence. Before we get into specifics, please allow a note of caution. It's important not to detract from your leadership presence by micromanaging your team to account for not seeing them every day. Managing your team remotely will put your trust propensity on full display. We'll review effective ways to monitor your team in the next chapter. For now, bear in mind that instant access was never possible – not even in the office. As your team works through the challenges of remote work, set realistic expectations around their accessibility and availability. Expect similar, but not more responsiveness than you would in an office environment. That said, to project leadership presence you'll need to layer a few things on top of availability, accessibility, and affinity. CTI research, referenced by Sylvia Ann Hewlett[1] in her book, Executive Presence reveals the top indicators of executive presence across several dimensions. Following are key results from that research and action plans for amplifying leadership presence. It focusses on refining how you act, how you communicate and how you appear.

1. **How you Act.** CTI research reveals that the top three indicators of how much weight, dignity, and importance a leader projects are their ability to project grace under fire, their decisiveness and their willingness to speak truth to power. Following are action plans to improve leadership presence relating to each indicator.

   <u>**Action Plans**</u>

   - **Project grace under fire.** To get better at projecting grace under fire, take a lesson from the Navy SEALS and practice tactical breathing. Slow your breathing rate by breathing through your nostrils and counting to four before each inhale and exhale. Next, take a lesson from bomb disposal experts and stay composed by focusing on what you can control. This tactic plays to your strengths and allows you to project confidence. In many cases, you can fix a problem quicker than you can identify the root causes. The quicker you can change the topic from "how did we get here?" to "what's the next step?", the better!

   - **Be Decisive.** Don't let great be the enemy of good. If a solution is good enough and time is short, consider going with it. It may be the best decision you can make under the time constraints. If the situation warrants, create an opt-out for yourself by saying something like, "Let's go with that solution for now and revisit it in a week." This will give you points on decisiveness and the option to upgrade the decision later. Another tactic is to develop your long-term strategy in advance. If a solution falls in line with it, approve it quickly. If it doesn't, reject it or approve it conditionally, pending corrections that comply with your long-term strategy.

   - **Speak truth to power.** if a leadership decision or plan doesn't make sense to you, say so in a respectful, diplomatic, collaborative manner. One of my favorite quotes is, "When two men in business agree on everything, one of them is unnecessary." Don't be unnecessary. Add the balancing perspective your leaders need to make the best decisions. Also, be willing to practice intelligent disobedience in the right situations. Don't blindly implement decisions that will clearly harm the team and the business. Factor in the information you have that decision makers may not be privy to or interested in. At times, you may decide to obey the spirit of a decision, but not the letter of it. At other times, you may decide to obey neither. For example, if you're mandated to do something unethical, this could harm the team and the business. Do your best to persuade your leaders to make the ethical choice. Notwithstanding, make an informed decision yourself. Be mindful of the political risks of disobeying a poor or unethical leadership decision (e.g., someone could inform the decision maker, or you could get fired) and the risks of obeying a poor or unethical leadership decision (e.g., you could get fired, lose the respect of your team, or go to jail). As anyone who has ever spoken truth to power can attest, there are no easy choices. The impact is considerable in terms of building leadership presence, but the consequences can be just as considerable.

2. **How you Communicate.** CTI research reveals that the top three indicators of how well a leader communicates are their speaking skills, their ability to command a room and their assertiveness. Following are action plans to improve leadership presence relating to each indicator.

<u>**Action Plan**</u>

- **Polish your Speaking Skills.** To polish your speaking skills, minimize verbal fillers (like "umm" and "uh"). Verbal fillers are more prevalent when you construct your thoughts in real time. One of the best ways to minimize them is to overprepare for your topic. Another is to anticipate surprises. Have you ever noticed how White House Press Secretaries answer some questions by reading a prepared script? This keeps them looking polished and prepared rather than off balanced and surprised. Finally, in remote environments, communication is trending toward written and away from verbal mediums. Therefore, it's important to also sharpen your grammatical skills. A good reference is On Writing Well, by William Zinsser[2].

- **Command the Virtual Room.** As with face-to-face meetings, the best thing you can do to command a virtual room is maintain eye contact. The only way to do this is to keep your eyes glued to your camera. This is difficult to do because you can't simultaneously keep your eyes glued to your camera and read the room. One work-around is to periodically disable your video. When you do this, be sure to post a professional headshot to maintain your image. Be very vocal while your camera is disabled so your team knows you're still engaged. For maximum engagement, it's a good idea to be on camera for the first and last 10-15 minutes of the meeting. The second important area is posture. Avoid slouching when running a meeting, as it distracts from your command of the virtual room. Select a chair that presents you in the most commanding position. Bar chairs with low backs work particularly well. They don't show up on camera and project an upright posture. Finally, configure your conferencing system to make a sound when someone enters or leaves the virtual room. Greet each person by name as they come and go. Personal recognition is more essential in virtual environments than in person.

- **Be Assertive.** When communicating virtually, to amplify leadership presence, you must assert command. This is less about doing all the talking and more about controlling the agenda and steering the conversation. Ironically, the less you talk, the more assertive you can appear. When you do speak, be direct and get to your point quickly. Summarize your main points and leave ample time for reactions from the team. The more your team interacts with your message, the less "Zoom fatigue" will set in. Another way to assert command is to maintain your leadership presence by quickly addressing challenges to your leadership. It's important to distinguish between constructive feedback and challenges to your leadership. If you are defensive toward constructive feedback, you can stifle innovation. Conversely, if you are passive toward challenges to your leadership, you can quickly lose command of a virtual team. Here are three ways to distinguish the two.

  - Constructive feedback helps you solve a problem, where leadership challenges focus on problems you can't solve.

- Constructive feedback enlists the team in support of your cause, where leadership challenges enlist the team against your cause.

- Constructive feedback searches for the root cause of the problem, where leadership challenges presume that you are the root cause of the problem.

Don't let challenges to your leadership go unaddressed. Ask your challenger to explain their position. Be sure to ask enough clarifying questions to assess the validity of their challenge. Then, calmly respond to the valid aspects of their challenge and correct the aspects that are off. Aggressive challengers may try to interrupt you and reinforce their position. Don't accommodate this interruption. Keep the floor until you're done. Be careful not to antagonize the challenger. Your goal is not to embarrass them but to assert your command over the team. Before you adjourn, ask the challenger to call you afterwards. This will send a clear message to the team that you're open to valid concerns but not to open challenges to your leadership. When the challenger calls you, do more questioning than talking. Discuss what you sensed during the meeting and ask for clarification. Be sure to remind them they can approach you directly if they have similar questions or feelings in the future.

3. **How you Appear.** CTI research reveals that the top three indicators of a favorable leadership image are a polished appearance, attractiveness/fitness, and professional clothing. Following are action plans to improve leadership presence relating to each indicator.

   <u>**Action Plan.**</u>

   - **Polish your Appearance.** As a leader, your professional image shouldn't take a hit because you're working from home. If your home office doesn't reflect your professionalism as well as the company office did, consider using a professional background image or video. Chapter 1 includes an exhaustive list of recommended equipment. In addition to these items, consider investing in a green screen to make your background image or video crisp. You don't have to settle for the standard backgrounds included with your conferencing platform. Online platforms like Adobe Stock, Storyblocks, or Shutterstock license a variety of professional images and video backgrounds. Remember, your goal is not just to appear professional, but to amplify your leadership presence. **Appendix B** includes specifications for uploading custom background images and videos for popular video conferencing platforms. Also, when you're giving a presentation, consider using two monitors. Use monitor A to keep an eye on your audience and monitor B to present your material. Be sure to keep your eyes on monitor A. Looking up at monitor B can make you look subservient and looking to the left or right at monitor B can make you look distracted.

- **Get Workout Voice.** My wife and I are into fitness. When either of us has gotten a workout and we speak by phone, the other person interrupts and says, "you have workout voice!" If you've ever spoken to someone within 1 or 2 hours of a workout, you can attest to this. What we mean by "workout voice" is, we can hear an attractive resonance, confidence and strength in their voice that wasn't there before the workout. Incorporating fitness into your day can help you project a more energetic and confident demeanor to your team.

- **Dress Professionally.** The professional image you built before the pandemic has been replaced with the image you are now projecting virtually. Dressing less professionally while working from home can create a more relaxed work environment, but it can also detract from your professional image. Even if your work culture is more relaxed, as a leader you should distinguish yourself as such. Take a screenshot of your next virtual meeting, send it to a confidant and ask who looks like the manager of the team. If they select someone other than you, ask why. Use their feedback to refine your professional image.

Emotional Intelligence and Presence

The emotional intelligence traits that can have the greatest impact on presence are Interpersonal Relationship Skills, Empathy and Social Responsibility. Following are definitions of each emotional intelligence trait, indicators of high and low effectiveness and steps you can take to improve.

Interpersonal Relationship Skills

Emotional closeness can make someone feel nearby when they're hundreds of miles away. Professionals who can close emotional distance and build strong relationships project a greater sense of presence when working from home. From an emotional intelligence standpoint, **interpersonal relationship skills** are evident when someone has the ability to develop and maintain mutually satisfying relationships that are characterized by trust and compassion. The following table includes indicators of high and low effectiveness using this emotional intelligence trait.

Low Effectiveness	High Effectiveness
• Unable to share feelings	• Comfortable sharing feelings
• Impersonal	• Comfortable in social situations
• Standoffish	• Maintains relationships over time

Earlier, we've provided steps you can take to amplify affinity, including finding meaningful common interests, taking a genuine interest in someone, and finding ways to collaborate. These are also ways to build and maintain interpersonal relationships. Three additional steps you can take are reading the room, being curious about your colleagues and speaking from the heart.

1. **Read the room.** Timely responses, relatable comments and sensitive perspectives are all byproducts of reading the room. By being observant, you can strike the right tone with colleagues and generate the type of spontaneous liking that builds rapport. Make a point to observe things like whether a colleague seems stressed, what their facial expression communicates about their reaction to an announcement or what position they tend to take in response to certain issues. When colleagues realize that you took the time to remember something personal about them – especially when you have no apparent motives – an opening for a mutually enjoyable interpersonal dynamic presents itself.

2. **Be curious.** Curiosity is the forerunner of genuineness. When you become genuinely curious about a favorable aspect of one of your colleagues, you have a head start toward building a good interpersonal dynamic. Almost everyone enjoys talking about their positive attributes or accomplishments. Asking simple questions like "what inspired you to run a marathon?" or "is this what you wanted to be when you grew up?" can work wonders. I'm reminded of an impactful conversation I had with a colleague. I had the distinct impression that he had previously worked at a much higher level. I asked him "to what extent does this position utilize your talents?". That led to a 2-hour conversation about our backgrounds, which strengthened our professional relationship.

3. **Speak from the heart.** The next tactic you can use to build interpersonal relationship skills is to speak from the heart. To speak from the heart is to say

something with non-surface emotional sincerity. People are naturally drawn to authenticity. You may have a different background from theirs, or an opposing viewpoint but if you speak from the heart, colleagues will generally respect you for it. Naturally, in a workplace setting, there are times when surface acting is needed to maintain professionalism and productivity. For example, it would be counterproductive to speak from the heart in the workplace on divisive topics that can take the focus away from delivering value to the business. Notwithstanding, remote workers who can find ways to balance professionalism with authenticity will build better synergy with colleagues. I'm reminded of a Database Architect I worked with. We couldn't be more different, and our teams were usually pitted against one another. Notwithstanding, we had an excellent dynamic because he gave honest feedback, and I always knew where he stood. Because of his forthright manner some of my colleagues felt he was "a strong cup of tea". If he couldn't accommodate a request, he said so, despite the escalations that often followed. Whatever people felt about his frank delivery, he was a popular and trusted figure because he spoke from the heart.

Empathy

Empathy is perhaps the most misunderstood, least utilized emotional intelligence trait. It's often confused with sympathy, which is the sorrow you feel for someone's misfortune. Sympathetic remarks begin with the word "I"; as in "I feel sorry for your loss". Empathetic remarks go a step further by demonstrating that you <u>understand</u> the feelings or perspective of another. They often begin with the word "you", as in "You must be furious right now." An empathetic statement used at the right moment can build rapport, diffuse conflicts, and pave the way for productive work relationships. For example, compare the following responses to a colleague who expresses disappointment over a missed deadline.

- **Frustrated Colleague:** "If I had known I couldn't rely on you, I would have asked someone else to do it. Have you any idea how high this can escalate?"

- **Response 1:** "Unreliable?! That's taking it a bit far, isn't it? I did the best I could under the circumstances. That's why we're always asking your team not to wait till the last minute to submit your requests."

- **Response 2:** "I'm sorry I didn't come through. I know what a bind this puts you in with senior management. Is there anything I can do to help explain the delay?"

Response 2 is much more effective at establishing presence by building affinity through empathy. Not only is it less defensive, but it also shows a clear understanding for the seat of the other party. This is a vital trait for remote workers. Sunil Prashara, President and CEO of the Project Management Institute (PMI) published a short video in July, 2020 titled Leading with Empathy[3]. In it, he posits that leaders who display empathy inspire teams and drive results. He describes empathy as one of the power skills project professionals need to emotionally connect with others when working remotely. From an emotional intelligence standpoint, **empathy** is the ability to recognize, understand and appreciate how other people feel. It involves being able to articulate your understanding of another's perspective and behaving in a way that is respectful of their feelings. The following table includes indicators of high and low effectiveness using this emotional intelligence trait.

Low Effectiveness	High Effectiveness
• Difficulty understanding people's feelings • Surprised by others' reactions • Difficulty relating to others	• Able to put on "others' shoes" • Anticipates others' reactions • Picks up on social cues

The best thing you can do to become more empathetic is postpone your response (emotional or rational) and focus entirely on reassuring the other party that you understand their position. You don't have to agree with their position. You just have to be able to understand it well enough to articulate it. By delaying your response, you will reassure the other party that you "know where they're coming from". This will give them the best incentive to make an effort to know where you're coming from. Take another look at Response 2 in the dialogue above. Can you see what's missing from this response? No explanation has been offered for the delay. The speaker has postponed both their emotions and their rationale until they have expressed empathy to the other party. The most likely follow-on response from the frustrated colleague is "I'm sorry I blew up at you. What happened, anyway?" By showing empathy, you can diffuse conflict and increase your sense of presence by building affinity with remote colleagues.

Social Responsibility

One of the misconceptions about working from home is that it limits opportunities to collaborate with others. While this may be true when the majority of the team works from the same physical location, this is the exception rather than the norm. Teams are increasingly geographically dispersed, which means a significant portion of the team is working remotely even when they're "in the office". Also, collaboration is less a product of teams working in proximity and more a product of teams comprised of team players. Team players are professionals with the emotional intelligence trait of social responsibility. From an emotional intelligence standpoint, **social responsibility** is the willingness to contribute to society, one's social group and the welfare of others. It involves acting responsibly, having social consciousness, and showing concern for the greater community. The following table includes indicators of high and low effectiveness using this emotional intelligence trait.

Low Effectiveness	High Effectiveness
• Unwilling to be involved with the team • Hesitant to commit to group activities • Low concern for others in the group • Behaves unethically	• Genuinely concerned for the welfare of teammates • Collaborative • Responsible and dependable • Behaves ethically

In the ground-breaking book The EQ Edge, Steven Stein and Howard Book[4] assert that social responsibility is the easiest component of emotional intelligence to change because unlike the others, it's directed outward. Becoming more socially responsible is a personal decision. Therefore, the best way to change it is to consider compelling reasons to do so. Following are four reasons to consider becoming more socially responsible.

1. **It feels good.** You have to experience some things to fully appreciate their impact. I'm reminded of a man I encountered who was experiencing homelessness. He was standing on a corner, holding up a sign which indicated that he was a veteran. I had twenty-two dollars in my wallet and had already

determined to give him two dollars. At the last minute, I considered that two dollars wouldn't go very far toward meeting his needs and gave him the twenty instead. To this day I can recall his heartfelt, grateful response. That man gave me much more than I gave him that day – a lesson in the gratifying nature of thoughtful giving. In workplace scenarios, even the smallest gestures can contribute greatly to the framework of social responsibility. They can build synergy and increase presence. For example, consider starting an initiative to collect funds for a co-worker's birthday gift or attending an optional meeting because you know your presence would encourage a teammate or the host.

2. **It can mend fences.** We've all done things we wish we could undo. Regretful actions have a reductive effect on self-regard. Though you can't erase the past, you can make efforts to create a better future. Sometimes we have a bad dynamic with a teammate, and we know exactly why. We know the exact issue, or past event that caused the rift. Maybe you and a teammate often complete for the spotlight, and this has diminished your rapport. Consider collaborating with them on an initiative where you can both shine. Maybe a colleague feels that you took all the credit for a project you both worked on. Make a point to highlight their contributions in the next team meeting. Demonstrating your concern for your colleague's well-being can positively impact your dynamic and the way you see yourself. As we'll discuss later, self-regard can also enhance your ability to inspire trust and close trust gaps.

3. **It reminds you of what's important.** In business environments where we're competing for advancement and market share, it's easy to lose sight of the more important aspects of life and work. When you take time to truly develop someone, help them solve a problem that will only benefit them or coach them through a difficult period, you get reminded that people are the most valuable part of any enterprise.

4. **It's the right thing to do.** One of my favorite Martin Luther King quotes is *"Cowardice asks the question, 'Is it safe?' Expediency asks the question, 'Is it politic?' Vanity asks the question, 'Is it popular?' But conscience asks the question, 'Is it right?' And there comes a time when one must take a position that is neither safe, nor politic, nor popular, but one must take it because one's conscience tells one that it is right."* Socially responsible deeds are the right things to do. They ensure that business value is not attained at the expense of

ethics or the surrounding environment.

Chapter Summary

In this chapter, we defined presence as the quality of being unseen, but present. We reviewed strategies for increasing your sense of presence by amplifying your availability (ability to be used), accessibility (ability to be reached) and affinity (ability to be felt). We discussed tactics for amplifying leadership presence, including improving how you act, how you communicate and how you appear. We concluded with strategies for increasing emotional intelligence in the areas of Interpersonal Relationship Skills, Empathy and Social Responsibility. For additional tactics, see **Appendix F** which includes an overview of the EQi-2.0 Emotional Assessment instrument and instructions for taking the assessment and learning where you should concentrate your efforts to become more effective.

References

1. Hewlett, Sylvia Ann. Executive Presence. Harper Collins, 2014.

2. Zinsser, William. On Writing Well. HarperCollins, 2006.

3. Project Management Institute (PMI). "Leading with Empathy" pmi.org, Sunil Prashara, July, 2020, https://www.pmi.org/about/leadership-governance/ceo-corner/unplugged-episode-12.

4. Stein, Steven and Book, Howard, Multi-Health Systems inc.. The EQ Edge. Jossey Bass, 2011.

3

Performance

The late Supreme Court Justice, Antonin Scalia wrote, "the main business of a lawyer is to take the romance, the mystery, the irony, the ambiguity out of everything he touches". This is what evaluators of performance should strive to do; remove the romance from evaluating favored employees, remove the mystery from the evaluation process, remove the irony by correctly distinguishing between appearance and reality, and remove the ambiguity by eliminating varying interpretations of the same performance results. No tool does this better than the SMART framework. Many professionals have memorized the acronym and even use it to some extent to craft goals, but few realize its full potential. To make remote work work, we must re-think our approach to performance by putting more rigor into the development, delivery and tracking of SMART goals.

Re-Thinking Performance

SMART goals are:

- **S**pecific – detailed versus general
- **M**easurable – able to be proven by relevant metrics
- **A**ttainable – realistic; achievable
- **R**elevant – aligned with larger strategic objectives
- **T**ime-based – deadline-driven; time-bound

When properly set, SMART goals will scare you. This is because they are trackable records of the specific ways you are committing to impact the business in a given business cycle. If you don't feel a tinge of fear after setting SMART goals, you haven't set them with enough specificity. They should motivate managers and teams to get busy making targets. Few professionals understand this better than Sales professionals. They're so confident in their ability to deliver that they often stake the lion's share of their salaries on it! They accept that if they don't perform quarter over quarter, they will be placed on probation. Instead of trying to curry favor with the boss to hide bad performance, they guarantee their longevity by delivering hard results. Why do we hold sales professionals to one standard and the rest of the business to another? Whatever the reason, these professionals prove that it's possible to impact the busines in measurable ways, quarter after quarter. And what do they gain from being held to such a high performance standard? In addition to being part of the small number of employees with profit-sharing agreements, their performance evaluation process is devoid of romance, mystery, irony, and ambiguity. They either make quota or they don't. My point is not to recommend that all parts of the business become quota-driven, but rather to highlight a clear example of using the SMART framework to its full potential. This framework has great utility in remote work applications. Once SMART goals are established, there's a clear understanding of expected performance results and less need for micromanagement. Business leaders should task themselves to identify the specific deliverables professionals should meet in a given business cycle and focus their management efforts on realizing those outcomes. Such an approach would increase business efficiency by minimizing busy work and maximizing results-oriented behaviors. The goal of this chapter is to help you realize the utility of the SMART framework when you're working remotely or managing remote workers. To do this, we'll focus on five universal performance measures you can use to deliver expected results or evaluate delivered results, irrespective of industry, profession or where the work is performed. We'll provide four examples of SMART goals under each performance measure that you can modify to make hard commitments for yourself or your team. We'll close this chapter by aggregating this information into concrete steps you can take to either deliver or monitor for optimal performance.

The five universal performance measures are:

- Quality

- Timeliness

- Quantity

- Communication

- Efficiency

Quality

Quality is the standard of someone's work outcome as compared with others, or the degree of excellence achieved. Performance results can be readily evaluated in terms of quality. One worker may have fewer complaints or more positive reviews than another. One project manager's report may be more complete and better formatted than another's. As a manager, you may be more inclined to showcase the work of one direct report over another's. These are indications of variable outcomes in terms of quality. To drive quality outcomes, professionals and managers should work together to establish SMART goals in terms of quality.

The following table includes four examples of SMART goals pertaining to **quality**.

Examples of SMART Quality Goals	
1	Reduce the number of year-over-year customer complaints by 50% by November 30, 20XX.
2	Increase the percentage of on-time deliveries by 10% by March 30, 20XX.
3	Increase the average customer satisfaction score to at least 80% by September 30, 20XX.
4	Reduce stock outs from 25% to less than 5% by June 30, 20XX

Timeliness

Timeliness is the delivery of a work product within a favorable or useful time frame. Like quality, it's a good, objective measure of performance. One worker completes required training on time, while another shows up regularly on the "naughty list" of employees who failed to do so. One engineer is regularly requested by project managers because they get work done faster. One manager's team is always "on the ball" when it comes to completing required training or getting projects closed out. These variations are often overlooked at review time – much to the dismay of professionals who work hard to distinguish themselves in the area of timeliness. To realize strategic initiatives like first-mover advantage, professionals and managers must work together to establish SMART goals around timeliness.

The following table includes four examples of SMART goals pertaining to **timeliness**.

Examples of SMART Timeliness Goals	
1	Close out 4 projects by September 30, 20XX.
2	Progress project X from 25% complete to 50% complete by June 30, 20XX.
3	Complete milestone X of project Y by March 30, 20XX.
4	Complete project X 30 calendar days faster than the average project delivery cycle of 10-months.

Quantity

Quantity is the sum of countable events or objects, expressed as a numerical value. It's the most obvious measure of performance. One project manager completes more projects per year than another. One system administrator configures more servers than another in a similar timeframe. One solution architect produces more designs than another on projects of similar complexity. In the post-COVID business world, teams will be required to do more with less. To do that, teams will need professionals who can do more with less – be it less time, less resources or less clarity. To identify and reward those professionals, leaders of teams will need to work with their professionals to establish SMART goals around quantity.

The following table includes four examples of SMART goals pertaining to **quantity**.

Examples of SMART Quantity Goals
1	Increase project load by 25% by June 30, 20XX by managing related projects as a program.
2	Increase the number of completed project by 25% over the prior year.
3	Reduce the total cost of project X by 20% as compared to project Y (which is similar in scope).
4	Save $100K across the entire project portfolio by 12/30/20XX by aggregating purchases and buying in bulk.

Communication

As a performance measure, communication can have a masking effect on all the others. The professional who is not timely but communicates well can appear timelier than they are. They can also appear to deliver better quality or a greater quantity of work than they actually do. Performance evaluators must resist the temptation to allow one performance measure to mask over another. Conversely, professionals that are being evaluated should perfect their communication skills. Doing so will not only cause this masking effect to work in their favor, but also improve leadership and overall effectiveness. The professional who communicates well attains better synergy with stakeholders, identifies root causes faster, keeps leaders and stakeholders informed and is easier to communicate with. Although it's apparent when someone communicates well, it's important for leaders and professionals to establish SMART goals around communication. This will minimize the masking effect and take ambiguity out of the evaluation process.

The following table includes four examples of SMART goals pertaining to **communication**.

Examples of SMART Communication Goals	
1	Complete a communication course by March 30, 20XX to improve communication and negotiation skills.
2	Migrate messaging from System X to System Y by June 30, 20XX to accommodate stakeholder communication preferences.
3	Develop, certify, and distribute uniform project status reports each week to all stakeholders, starting on May 1, 20XX.
4	Distribute project meeting minutes within 48 hours of meeting, starting February 1, 20XX.

Efficiency

As a performance measure, efficiency is the ability to manage multiple tasks simultaneously. It's the essence of working smarter and not harder. There's always a hint of innovation in the efficient professional, enabling them to achieve higher levels of performance with fewer resources. In the post-COVID business world, smart managers will place a premium on efficient workers. One project manager will complain about being overloaded while another manages higher workloads by managing projects with similar resources as a program. One manager complains there is no training budget while another challenges her team to research, develop and deliver in-house training on the latest technological trends. One system administrator spins up 8 virtual environments in the time another spins up 3. These variations are not accidental and shouldn't be overlooked at review time. They're the result of using thought work and dedication to overcome resource limitations.

The following table includes four examples of SMART goals pertaining to **efficiency**.

Examples of SMART Efficiency Goals
1	By September 30, 20XX, participate in cross-training to learn other roles so that critical functions are covered during absences.
2	By June 30, 20XX, increase project workload by 25% by managing 5 newly assigned projects as a program, using the same project resources.
3	By March 30, 20XX, incorporate RPA to generate automatic system up-dates, thereby reducing 20 hours of work per week across the entire team.
4	By June 30, 20XX, deliver cross-training to boundary partners to improve communications.

How to Deliver Optimal Performance

The key to delivering optimal performance is clearly defining what it is. Remove romance, mystery, irony, and ambiguity from the evaluation process by defining SMART goals around universal performance measures like the ones we've just reviewed. If you're reluctant to commit yourself to such lofty, specific goals consider the alternatives. You could otherwise be held accountable for hitting subjective, ambiguous, moving targets. By setting goals that are specific, measurable, attainable, relevant, and time-bound, you can dedicate an entire performance cycle to exceeding them. SMART goals are not subject to how your boss feels about you at review time or whether your manager has been supervising you long enough to know your performance history. Even a relatively new manager can assess whether you've met or exceeded a SMART goal. Here are three steps you can take to deliver indisputable optimal performance.

1. Set smart SMART goals

2. Under promise and over deliver

3. Use your boss wisely

Set smart SMART goals

If you haven't established SMART goals with your manager, start gathering data and launch a plan to establish them. SMART goals are like a contract. You meet the terms of the agreement, fall short of them, or exceed them. It's impossible to prove that you've exceeded a target like "just do a good job". If your manager is very informal, establish your SMART goals in an informal manner.

To do so, get answers to questions like:

- What's an objective measure of my performance last year?

- What's an objective measure of my peer's performance last year?

- What's my manager's idea of a good, great, or awesome job?

- What aspects of my job can I quantify?

  - Do I manage a certain number of projects?

  - Do I configure a certain number of devices?

  - Do I process a certain number of applications?

  - Do I typically process tasks within a certain number of weeks?

- What quantifiable aspect of my job can I improve?

- Are there dashboards that I can use to determine the average throughput of my peers?

- What work outcome(s) is my manager most concerned about?

- What are the trouble spots on my team?

- If I had to hire a consultant to do my job, what criteria would I use to evaluate them?

- What SMART goals can I establish around Quality, Timeliness, Quantity, Communication and Efficiency?

Here's something to note. When establishing your SMART goals, be fair to yourself. Don't inadvertently create a higher performance standard for yourself than the team is being held to (unless, of course you negotiate compensation for it!). The idea is to establish an objective way to highlight the value you bring to the team and how that value is appreciating over time. The establishment of SMART goals should be a collaborative effort between you and your manager. If done correctly, it will become a team performance standard that can be used to easily distinguish between good, great, and awesome performance.

Under promise and over deliver

There's a trustworthy business maxim that reads "under promise and over deliver". Good lawyers have a rendition that reads "never ask a question you don't know the answer to". The objective of both is to guarantee your desired outcome by only venturing down predictable paths. That begins with project selection and data analysis. For example, before committing to delivering a project 30 days faster than the typical delivery cycle, make sure you've identified the means by which you will compress the schedule. Before committing to closing four projects by the end of the 3rd quarter, make sure you've got at least six candidate projects, four of which can possibly close by the middle of the 2nd quarter. Before committing to save $100K across an entire project portfolio by end of year, make sure you've spoken with your vendors to confirm your bulk buying discount can deliver that amount of savings. The idea is not to *deliver* less than you're able to, but rather to *promise* to deliver less than you're able to. After putting your commitment in writing, do everything you can to exceed it. Don't relax because your goal appears to be guaranteed. Even the most reliable estimates are subject unforeseen risks.

Use your boss wisely

One of the most underutilized resources is the recurring one-on-one meeting between direct-report and manager. While it is true that these meetings can build rapport or surface issues that may not otherwise appear, there's a general tendency to deemphasize their primary advantage – to ensure performance targets are met or exceeded. If you have a monthly one-on-one meeting with your boss, then you have twelve opportunities throughout the year to solicit the help of a powerful ally to resolve issues preventing you from exceeding your SMART goals. As it happens, this ally is the very person who will rate your performance at the end of the year. At the beginning of the year, clarify your intent to exceed your SMART goals with your manager. This is a subtle, effective way of stating that you are expecting and willing to work for an **Exceed** rating come review time. Think of your monthly one-on-one meetings as twelve opportunities to course correct. During these meetings, you should have a clear idea where you should be in terms of meeting your goals and deliberately engage your manager about removing performance obstacles. Each month, you should be 1/12th of the way to your goal. For example, if your goal is to save $100K by end of year, you should have saved $16.6K by your second monthly meeting. This of course assumes your spend rate is even throughout the year. Notwithstanding, these meetings are your opportunities to enlist your manager in steadily progressing towards your goals. If you have several one-on-one meetings per month, then you have more opportunities to course-correct before review time. Think of your boss as a client from whom you're hoping to win a big contract. Not only will this client award the contract, but they're also willing to help you win it! Would you ever meet with this client and not discuss how you could improve your standing? Your boss is the sole awardee of the coveted **Exceed** rating. This rating is reserved for workers who can best demonstrate that they've earned it. Therefore, use your recurring one-on-one meetings to demonstrate that you're earning it.

Here's a final note. Although It's rare to exceed all your SMART goal targets and fail to get an **Exceed** rating, this is entirely possible. It happened to me once. Afterwards, I had a lengthy discussion with my manager. She explained that I was a top contender for the rating, but leadership had mandated that only a select few could get it. When I asked why I was not included in that number, she explained that it was based upon the relative impact my projects had on the business. I kept a cool demeanor and asked that in the future, I be given projects that had a greater impact on the business. The very next year, I received the **Exceed** rating. The moral of the story is there's no downside to exceeding your SMART goals. In fact, the year I failed to get the **Exceed** rating, I also failed to make the list of employees that were laid off. I was shooting for the moon and landed among the stars.

Smart Monitoring

According to the 6th edition of the Project Management Body of Knowledge (PMBOK), the likelihood of project success is greatly increased if processes are invoked to initiate, plan, execute, monitor, control, and close projects. The monitoring and controlling processes are not arbitrary checkpoints to appease managers with a low propensity to trust. They are meant to collect performance data and track, review and regulate progress toward stated objectives. Remote employee monitoring should achieve similar objectives. Smart monitoring is about helping direct reports meet or exceed their SMART goals. If you only meet with them once per month, you'll only have twelve opportunities to guarantee their success. If you only discuss what's on their mind, you may build rapport, but you'll miss an opportunity to guide their progress toward stated objectives.

Smart monitoring has four characteristics.

1. It has a clear objective

2. It avoids overhelping

3. It checks for both performance and infractions

4. It's frequent enough to course correct

Have a Clear Objective

Consider the following scenarios.

Scenario 1

A project manager needs to ensure a critical task gets done by Friday. On Monday, he gets a commitment from his resource that the task will be finished by Friday, as requested. What's the project manager's best course of action?

    A. Wait till Friday and assume the resource will keep their word.

    B. Check with the resource multiple times each day to ensure they're on track.

    C. Check with the resource in the middle of the week to build rapport.

    D. Check with the resource in the middle of the week to ask for status and ask how he can help ensure success.

Scenario 2

A manager's goal is to ensure her team implements a strategic objective by the end of the year. In January, she establishes SMART goals with her team in support of this objective. Each direct report commits to delivering their portion of the work by the end of the year. What's her best course of action?

    A. Wait till the performance review period at the end of the year and assume her direct reports will have met their SMART goals.

    B. Check in on her staff multiple times daily to ensure they're on track.

C. Establish recurring one-one-one meetings to build rapport throughout the year.

D. Establish recurring one-one-one meetings to build rapport throughout the year, check status and ask how she can help ensure success.

In both scenarios, option D is clearly the best choice. Option A has the semblance of trust but it's not the type of trust that inspires optimal performance. In fact, it may inspire the opposite. We'll discuss the type of trust that inspires optimal performance in the Chapter 4. Option B helps the team, but also hurts the team. It provides more help than is necessary to complete the work and consequently, can leave work that does require management support unsupported. It guarantees business outcomes at the expense of worker morale and autonomy. Option C misconstrues the purpose of the team as building synergy, rather than delivering value to the business. Option D is the correct approach because it underscores that the objective of one-one-one meetings and all monitoring efforts, is to assist employees in their quest to meet or exceed SMART performance targets.

Consider dividing end-of-year SMART goal metrics into quarterly, monthly, or weekly targets. Be sure to allow for uneven delivery cycles. For example, some goals will go from 10% complete to 100% complete in a single day. Notwithstanding, checkpoint targets are a good way to keep you and your direct reports focused on the business objectives. If they fall behind schedule, your goal is to help them course correct or perhaps encourage them to be patient and keep doing what they're doing until the course corrects itself.

Avoid Overhelping

The National Basketball Association (NBA) has coined the phrase "overhelping". It describes when a defender leaves their primary duties to provide help where help is not needed. The result is an opposing player is left undefended and has a good chance of scoring. In the workplace, we call this micromanagement. We joke about it and acknowledge that all professionals do it to some extent. But we often underestimate its erosive effect on performance. Smart monitoring helps only where help is needed. Reviewing policies that are already clear, approving routine correspondence that could have been disseminated days ago or hosting meetings to review information that could have been read in a report are all examples of overhelping. A good rule of thumb is to ask whether a planned activity will progress the individual or the team toward meeting their SMART goals. If not, consider replacing it with an activity that does.

Monitor for both Performance and Infractions

Monitoring for infractions is as important as monitoring for performance. It's the essence of the phrase trust but verify. Many leaders have fallen from great heights for allowing things to happen "on their watch". To avoid joining their ranks, make sure you're watching. The remote workforce presents unique challenges in the area of employee monitoring. Use the systems at your disposal to detect and deal with infractions. Be mindful that no employee monitoring system is as effective as your instincts. Investigate hunches and clarify suspicions. No employee wants to be monitored until a fellow employee breaks the rules. That's when they'll assert "there should be systems in place to catch stuff like this". In other words, "someone should be monitoring us to ensure stuff like this doesn't happen". It's important for remote workers to feel that you're watching—Not only to detect infractions, but also to boost morale. Few things decrease productivity faster than the feeling that no one is watching anyway. That said, when you monitor for infractions be quick to give the benefit of the doubt. Bear in mind that lengthy idle times could be perfectly legitimate. Remote workers may use the quiet, uninterrupted time at home to work on project schedules or write reports, which can appear as idle time. Encourage your team to use presence indicators to broadcast their activities, to give stakeholders the assurance that they can be reached if needed. In closing, the goal of monitoring for infractions is to deter the small percentage of employees that will violate policy, without causing the majority of employees that won't to feel untrusted.

Be Frequent Enough to Course Correct

Another reason option A was incorrect in the two scenarios presented earlier, is that performance discussions were too infrequent to help the team meet their performance targets. Your coaching should be frequent enough for course correction and infrequent enough for employee development and discovery. It should also factor in the development level of the team. Contrast the coaching styles of Phil Jackson of the 2001 Lakers and "Coach K" (Mike Krzyzewski) of the Duke Blue Devils. The following sketch captures Phil Jackson's style perfectly.

His players were seasoned professionals, and his interventions were infrequent during basketball quarters. That season, he would wait until deep into most quarters to call time outs. The player to his right is Derek Fisher, who later became president of the NBA Players Association and a coach himself. Jackson's coaching interventions were frequent enough to affect the outcome of games and infrequent enough to allow the players to develop a feel for the system they were implementing. This is evidenced by the 11 NBA titles he won as a coach, surpassing the previous record of 9 by Red Auerbach.

The sketch below is a good reflection of the coaching the style of "Coach K" of the Duke Blue Devils.

You won't find as much player interaction on his sideline because he's not only coaching players, but he's also developing them. As such, his interventions are more frequent than Phil Jackson's were in the prior example. Notwithstanding, all his interventions are purposeful. They significantly impact the outcome of the game and in his case, the development of the players. This is evidenced by the 5 national championships he's won and the 14 players he's sent to the NBA. Despite their differences, both coaches intervened only as frequently as required to achieve their objectives. Their interventions were not driven by a low propensity to trust or a need for control. They were driven by a laser focus on results.

Emotional Intelligence and Performance

All emotional intelligence traits can positively impact performance. That said, the ones that are particularly meaningful in the context of remote work performance are Self-Actualization, Assertiveness and Optimism. Following are definitions of each emotional intelligence trait, indicators of high and low effectiveness and steps you can take to improve.

Self-Actualization

The late Kobe Bryant was the embodiment of self-actualization. In the book *Mamba Mentality*[1], Phil Jackson describes his first encounter with Kobe Bryant as follows. "Kobe wanted to impress upon me how happy he was to have the opportunity to play in the triangle system – and how much he already knew about it… Here he was, 20 years old, sounding like he'd been a pro for a decade." At the time of this encounter, Phil Jackson had just won his sixth NBA championship with the Chicago Bulls. Many players would have expressed excitement simply to *play* for Phil Jackson. Kobe wanted to play in his *system*. At a young age, he had a clear idea how he wanted to impact not only his team, but also the game of basketball in general. He had a strong drive to win. Kobe Bryant would have significantly impacted the game of basketball, irrespective which team he played for. Similarly, remote workers who are strong in self-actualization will deliver optimal performance, irrespective where they perform the work. From an emotional intelligence standpoint, **self-actualization** is the ability to realize your potential capacities. It's the willingness to persistently try to improve yourself and pursue meaningful objectives that lead to a richer, more fulfilling life. The following table includes indicators of high and low effectiveness using this emotional intelligence trait.

Low Effectiveness	High Effectiveness
• Unmotivated • Needs handholding • No long-term goals	• Clear short-term and long-term goals • Highly motivated • Passionate and enthusiastic

Self-Actualization is largely a question of motivation. In fact, the term was popularized by motivation theorist Albert Maslow. In his book *A Theory of Human Motivation*[2], he writes "Whereas the average individuals often have not the slightest idea of what they are, of what they want, of what their own opinions are, self-actualizing individuals have superior awareness of their own impulses, desires, opinions, and subjective reactions in general." This quote contains three clues for increasing self-actualization, including finding your passion, finding your strengths, and making a To-*Don't* list.

- **Find your passion.** Despite graduating as an engineering major from one of the top five engineering schools, I spent the majority of my professional life managing projects and teaching leadership courses. I learned early in my career that though I had been educated to be an engineer, I lacked the passion. I was much more interested in work that involved interacting with people. I'm reminded of my first engineering job at a utility company. I was responsible for developing plans to relocate our gas lines in response to municipal road improvement projects. I found greater satisfaction negotiating with city representatives to find ways to **not** move our gas lines, than developing designs to move them. The bigger the pipes, the stronger my negotiating position and the better chance I had of negotiating my way out of having to move them. By contrast, some of my peers longed for the opportunity to develop plans to move the big pipes. The bigger the pipes, the more excited they would be about moving them. The difference between my passion to do the true engineering work and theirs was my first clue that my passions lied elsewhere. When I discovered the field of project management, my passions awakened. I could negotiate to my heart's content, interact with various departments and levels of leadership, and put my technical acumen to use on technical projects. To spark your drive to self-actualize, find your passion. You don't always have to change careers as I did to find it. Find ways to incorporate your passions into the work you're doing now. Do you like designing? Propose a new design for a weekly report your team sends out. Do you like to teach? Learn about a new, relevant technology and volunteer to train the team on it. Finding ways to incorporate your passions into the work you're currently doing can make a 10-hour workday feel like a 6-hour workday.

- **Find your strengths.** One of the unfortunate things about trending business ideas is that once the fad is over, the business world abandons the idea altogether and deems it passe. This is unfortunate because some of the most valuable and relevant insights are tucked away in books that have been long forgotten. One such work is *Now, Discover your Strengths*[3], by Marcus Buckingham and Donald Clifton. It includes access to an assessment you can take to discover strengths you may be unaware of. The premise of the book is that it is better to focus on your strengths than your weaknesses. Finding and showcasing your strengths in your current role can increase your level of engagement (everyone likes doing what they're good at!) and give you a permanent competitive edge. For example, if you're naturally attentive to details, someone would have a difficult time competing against you as an auditor or an accountant.

- **Make a To-*Don't* List.** A To-Don't list is a list of behaviors and practices that sap energy, decrease motivation, divert focus, waste time, or make you feel bad about yourself. Such a list is helpful if you want to maintain a productive flow and in the words of Maslow "superior awareness of your subjective reactions in general".

Here's a sample To-*Don't* List to get you started.

✓ Don't respond to an offensive or provocative remark

✓ Don't get pulled into a topic you've decided to avoid

✓ Don't allow an unqualified person or low-priority issue to redirect your focus or energy

✓ Don't accept a suspicious invitation

✓ Don't agree with something disagreeable

✓ Don't make a big deal out of every big deal

✓ Don't respond sooner than you're prepared to

Assertiveness

Comments like *"People see you as more of a behind the scenes person."* and *"Your name never comes up when people think about the next wave of leaders"* and *"That's a great idea. You should have spoken up!"* are all indicators of a lack of assertiveness. These sorts of comments can make their way into your performance reviews and limit your advancement opportunities. A lack of assertiveness has always been a career limiter and it is even more so in remote environments, where your contributions to the business are not as evident. From an emotional intelligence standpoint, **assertiveness** is the ability to express your thoughts, opinions, ideas, feelings, and beliefs and defend yourself without becoming aggressive or abusive.

The following table includes indicators of high and low effectiveness using this emotional intelligence trait.

Low Effectiveness	High Effectiveness
• Passive	• Comfortable expressing themselves
• Rarely contributes ideas	• Direct
• Quick to defer to others, accommodate or compromise	• Defends themselves in a non-destructive manner
• Doesn't defend themselves	• Not overly controlled or outwardly shy

The decision to become more assertive is just that, a decision. The best way to make such a decision is to consider compelling reasons to do so. Here are three considerations for your consideration.

1. **Consider the root causes.** There's a reason people decide to be non-assertive. They may view deferring to others as the higher and nobler path. They may view it as a way to mitigate conflict. Perhaps their role in the organization could be associated with non-assertive behavior, and therefore they may feel pressure to conform to the expectations of the role. They could be unassertive because their over-impressed with the qualifications of others and under-impressed with their own qualifications. Incidentally, this is precisely what some of their competitors want them to feel! Finally, they could be modeling the non-assertive behavior of their leader, parent, or role model. Whatever the root cause, identifying it is the first step in deciding to become more assertive.

2. **Consider your rights.** One of the subtler negative consequences of non-assertive behavior is that it not only defers to the thoughts, feelings, and opinions of others, but it can defer your rights as well. Here's a list of some assertive rights everyone is entitled to, irrespective of role or rank:

   - The right to express feelings, ideas, opinions, and values.

   - The right to change your mind.

   - The right to make decisions.

   - The right to say, "I don't know".

   - The right to say, "I don't understand".

   - The right to say "no", without feeling bad or guilty.

   - The right to be yourself.

   - The right to privacy.

   - The right to be alone.

   - The right to be independent.

   - The right to reject someone's advice.

   - The right to be non-assertive.

As you reflect on your workplace and social dynamics, do you feel that you have deferred any of these rights? If so, this could indicate that you should decide to be more assertive.

3. **Consider the benefits of assertive behavior.** The following list of benefits of assertive behavior was modified from a list published by the Mayo Clinic[4]. Following are explanations of each benefit.

- **Gain more self-confidence.** Assertive behavior will allow you to vet your ideas with others and gain confidence in the credibility of your contributions.

- **Understand your feelings better.** Sometimes you can't fully understand your feelings until you attempt to describe them and let others interact with them. This interaction will help you pinpoint what you're feeling and refine how you express them.

- **Earn respect from others.** Assertive behavior earns respect from others by ensuring they factor your thoughts, preferences, and ideas into decisions. It reinforces that your concurrence is not automatic, and that no decision will be final until it has the benefit of your input, which is a sign of respect.

- **Improve communications.** When you assert yourself, people will know what you're thinking or feeling. This will reduce communication disconnects by minimizing assumptions and clarifying expectations.

- **Create win-win outcomes.** When you assert yourself, you fully express your own concerns and make room for the concerns of others. Win-win outcomes are only possible if all concerns (including yours!) are on the table.

- **Improved Decision-Making.** You have a seat at the table for a reason. Someone felt you had something valuable to contribute. Honor their faith in you by contributing your ideas and perspectives. Ironically, the ideas and perspectives of non-assertive persons are often the most impactful. This is because they spend so much time reading the room and listening to others that their thoughts are usually the most original and informed.

- **Honest Relationships.** When you assert yourself, people will learn what you really think and get to know you better. They'll discover surprising things about you that may challenge their initial assumptions. This level of intimacy can be intimidating to some, but it's the only way to build honest work relationships.

- **Greater Job Satisfaction.** Assertive behavior is engaged behavior. When you engage more, the work will become more fulfilling. Often, it's not so much the work that makes a job fulfilling as it's the people you're collaborating with to perform the work.

Optimism

Optimism is the emotional intelligence trait that can give you the courage to set aggressive SMART goals and inspire the confidence of your leaders and stakeholders that you will meet or exceed them. It's an infectious trait that can build confidence in others and cause them to perform better than they thought they could. Even when optimists face setbacks, they're quick to make plans to work around them. From an emotional intelligence standpoint, **optimism** is a positive attitude and perspective. It involves remaining positive and resilient in the face of setbacks. The following table includes indicators of high and low effectiveness using this emotional intelligence trait.

Low Effectiveness	High Effectiveness
• Difficulty seeing the good • Fears the worst will happen • Pessimistic about the future	• Sees possibilities • Hopeful approach toward adversity and life in general • Confident about the future

Before reviewing ways to become more optimistic, it's important to dispel a popular misconception about it. Optimism is not the ability to think that everything will turn out well in the end. It's the ability to disrupt yourself from thinking unproductive thoughts when things don't go as planned. In his book, Learned Optimism[4], Martin Seligman distinguishes optimists from pessimists by their ability to disrupt themselves from viewing negative events as pervasive, permanent, or entirely their fault.

Following are tips for avoiding these three pitfalls and becoming more optimistic.

1. **It's almost never Pervasive.** Pessimistic people exaggerate the pervasiveness of negative events. While it's important to have a realistic view of potential risks, it's also important to have a realistic assessment about the pervasiveness of a negative event. For example, a company may announce layoffs, but they may be confined to parts of the business that are in decline. It would be a mistake to distract yourself with anxiety if you're in the growth part of the business. Even if you are in an impacted part of the business, bear in mind that according to the US Bureau of Labor Statistics, the average layoff rate has hovered around 15% for the past five years. That means 85% of workers are successful at competing for their jobs and surviving layoffs. My point is not to paint a rosy picture, especially in the post-COVID business world, but rather to encourage realism over pessimism and productive thoughts over unproductive ones. As bad as things may get, problems are almost never as pervasive as pessimists can make them out to be.

2. **It's almost never Permanent.** Pessimists are quick to believe problems and setbacks are permanent. This belief is problematic because it can cause them to give up too quickly or discourage them from developing a solution to the problem. Optimists tend to believe that problems are temporary setbacks. This belief inspires persistence and innovative solutions. A great example of this is when the 1993 Buffalo Bills overcame a 32-point deficit to beat the Houston Oilers in overtime. The Bills were down 28–3 at halftime. Despite playing an exceptional team that had recently beaten them 27–3, they refused to believe their opponent's lead was permanent and made the biggest comeback in NFL history. That win is so well-known that it's often simply referred to as "The Comeback." Take a lesson from the 1993 Buffalo Bills and make your opponents (i.e., setbacks) prove that they can defeat you.

3. **It's almost never entirely your fault.** The third thought pattern that distinguishes optimists from pessimists is that pessimists tend to shoulder all the blame when bad things happen, thereby reinforcing a defeatist or victim mentality. While optimists may embrace that there may have been things they could have done differently, they are quicker to share the blame with other credible causes. The next time you're inclined to shoulder all the blame for a mistake or setback, consider other credible causes like inefficient processes,

unproductive work cultures and unsupportive stakeholders. The goal of this tactic is not to shift blame, but to protect an important tool (your optimism and confidence) in solving the dilemma.

Chapter Summary

In this chapter, we prescribed using the SMART framework as a management tool to rethink performance. We applied it to five universal performance measures that can be used to deliver or evaluate results, irrespective of industry, profession or where the work is performed. The five universal performance measures we reviewed are Quality, Timeliness, Quantity, Communication and Efficiency. We then aggregated this information into concrete steps you can take to either deliver optimal performance or use smart monitoring to help workers meet performance targets. We concluded with strategies for increasing emotional intelligence in the areas of Self-Actualization, Assertiveness and Optimism. For additional tactics, see **Appendix C** which includes 10 tips for battling "Zoom Fatigue" and **Appendix D** for 12 things you can expect as workers head back to the office.

References

1. Bryant, Kobe. Mamba Mentality. MCD Books, 2018.

2. Malow, Albert. A Theory of Human Motivation. WatchMaker Publishing, 1943.

3. Buckingham, Mark and Clifton, Donald. Now, Discover Your Strengths. The Free Press, 2001.

4. Mayo Clinic. "Stressed out? Be assertive" mayoclimic.org, Mayo Clinic Staff, 05/29/20, https://www.mayoclinic.org/healthy-lifestyle/stress-management/in-depth/assertive/art-20044644.

5. Seligman, Martin. Learned Optimism. 2006.

4

Trust

I n his best-selling book, Speed of Trust[1], Stephen Covey defines trust as the sum of character and competence. Someone may be an excellent lawyer but unless you perceive them to be upstanding and responsible you won't be inclined to ask them to watch over your children. Conversely, you may assess someone's character as honest, responsible, and fair but unless they have the relevant competence, you won't be inclined to have them be your pilot. We will hold to Covey's premise and expand on the definition of trust.

Trust is the lubricant that makes remote work work. Without it, teams will conceal mistakes, fail to ask for guidance, jump to conclusions about the intentions of others, over-rely on surface appearances, deemphasize the skills and accomplishments of others, waste time managing behaviors for effect and avoid one another. These behaviors are all nonstarters in a post-COVID world where business leaders are endeavoring to digitally transform businesses, gain first mover advantage, accelerate the commercialization of promising technology, and implement viable post-COVID business models. To accomplish these things, organizations must operate at a speed that is only possible in high-trust environments. In this chapter, we'll define trust and identify ways to close trust gaps between managers and the professionals they supervise by earning and extending the right kind of trust.

Trust Quadrants

Trust is a firm belief in the reliability, truth, ability, or strength of someone. Whether you have had positive or negative trust experiences is largely attributable to how or whether you arrive at this firm belief. If you trust based on sufficient probing, then you tend to extend **safe trust** and your trust experiences have likely been positive. If you trust based on insufficient probing, then you tend to extend **unprotected trust** and your trust experiences have likely been negative. These experiences can help explain how others have fared in their endeavors to earn your trust. There are four possible trust scenarios. In the first scenario, you're quick to trust and slow to probe. Almost everyone earns your trust from the start. In the second scenario, you're slow to trust and quick to probe. No one earns your trust from the start, and few earn it in the end. In the third scenario, you're slow to trust and slow to probe, which means you're indifferent about trust and probably transactional in your dealings. You've likely been burned so often or so badly by misappropriated trust that you don't even bother examining a person's trustworthiness anymore. In the fourth scenario, you're both quick to trust and quick to probe. You want to trust but you want others to be good stewards of the trust you extend them.

Here is a graphical depiction of each scenario. Going forward, we'll refer to each trust scenario as a Trust Quadrant.

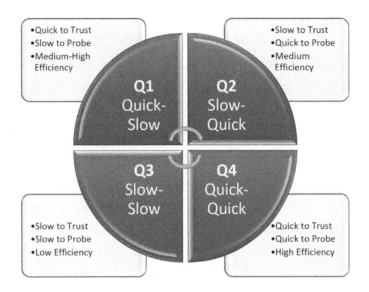

Trust is one of the highest hurdles to scale when working remotely. The key to scaling it is learning to earn the trust of managers and direct reports in each trust quadrant. The reward is higher efficiency, which minimizes the waste of energy, money, and time in producing desired results.

Earning Trust

The first person's trust you must earn is your own. If you commit to a work-out program, do you believe you will follow through with it? If you commit to earning a certification, do you believe you will earn it? If you enroll in a course, do you believe you will complete it and master the relevant skills? All emotional intelligence models emphasize that you must first be able to assess your own emotions before you can accurately assess others. The same applies to trust. You must first be able to earn your own trust before you can earn the right kind of trust from others. In this section, we'll discuss how to earn trust from yourself and then from professionals in each trust quadrant.

Earning Your Own Trust

You know when someone is likely to follow through and when they're likely to flake. You know the same about yourself. Think about something you absolutely know you will do today, like going to work or school. You know you may face obstacles but there's no doubt that you'll be there.

Now, consider that not everyone has that much self-trust. Someone struggling with a chemical dependency may need to set a smaller goal. They may need to simply commit to getting up at an agreed upon time. The point is, wherever you are in the self-trust spectrum the first step is the same. Start with small goals that you have a high probability of achieving. For example, if you have difficulty completing a 12-week continuing education course, commit to completing a 2-hour on-demand course. If you can't commit to earning a certification, commit to earning a badge for completing a training program at work. If you're unlikely to follow through on a running regimen, commit to a walking regimen. As you follow through on small commitments to yourself, you'll build the self-trust you need to follow through on commitments you make to others.

Earning Trust from Managers in the QUICK-SLOW Trust Quadrant

Managers in the first trust quadrant **(Quick-Slow)** are quick to trust and slow to probe. They're more impacted by the promises of trust than its liabilities. They're often agreeable and easy to work for. Because they trust so easily, it can be tempting to earn the wrong kind of trust from them. It's important to realize the distinction between being easily persuaded to believe something and having a lack of good sense or judgement. Managers in the Quick-Slow quadrant don't lack good sense or judgement. Their high propensity to trust is often shaped by their outlook. They often extend trust quickly because they want to give people a chance to prove them wrong (or right!). Work just as hard to earn their trust as you would anyone else's. Consider that earning their trust and keeping it are two different things. Demonstrate that you intend to keep their trust by being honest, respectful, and trustworthy.

Be Honest

Always be honest with managers in the Quick-Slow (or any) trust quadrant. This will prolong their trust in you. Let them know where you stand on issues, especially when they have an opposing view. They'll be refreshed by your authenticity and may be open to taking another view. Don't try to manipulate them or take their trust for granted. Anything gained too easily can be lost just as easily.

Be Respectful

Some find it difficult to genuinely respect managers who trust too easily. Like love, respect is impossible to fake. You either have it or you don't. Therefore, invest time getting to know managers that fit into the Quick-Slow trust quadrant. Learn about them and learn from them. Why are they so inclined to trust? What experiences or thought processes contributed to their outlook? How can their perspective expand your own? Earnest curiosity can work wonders in terms of building respect for someone with a different outlook. Also, by building genuine respect, you will have met one of their greatest needs. Since it can be difficult to genuinely respect managers that trust too easily, some don't bother trying.

Be Trustworthy

Being trustworthy with a high-trust manager sends a strong, clear message *"I don't want something from you that I haven't earned"*. You'll earn a deeper and more abiding kind of trust from them. Quick-Slow managers are eager to realize the promise of trust. They're policy is like the return policy at Nordstrom's. Unlike some department stores, Nordstrom realizes that only 6% of the population is willing to return something they shouldn't. That gives 94% of us a great shopping experience. If you work for a Quick-Slow manager, don't be part of the 6%. Earn their trust as you would anyone else's.

Earning Trust from Direct Reports in the QUICK-SLOW Trust Quadrant

Direct Reports in the first trust quadrant **(Quick-Slow)** are quick to trust and slow to probe. They're more impacted by the promises of trust than its liabilities. They're often agreeable and easy to work with. Because they trust so easily, it can be tempting to take their trust for granted. Don't yield to this temptation. As mentioned earlier, earning their trust and keeping it are two different things. Be sure to put in the work required to keep their trust by being honest, respectful, and trustworthy.

Be Honest

One of the most difficult aspects of leadership is having difficult conversations, like why you rated one direct report higher than another, why an ambitious worker is not ready for more responsibility, or what growth areas a defensive direct report must work on to be more effective. If a direct report has already given you their trust, honor it by being honest and clear about what may be holding them back. Some managers try to preserve rapport by being vague on such topics, sugarcoating the truth or balancing unpleasant truths with pleasant truths. These tactics run the risk of obfuscating your message and could harm the trust dynamic. As uncomfortable as it may be at times, honesty is really the best policy. Quick-Slow direct reports won't always like or agree with what you have to say, but they'll be reassured that you will be honest with them and call things the way you seem them.

Be Respectful

The squeaky wheel gets the grease. This is an unfortunate reality when it comes to working with Quick-Slow direct reports. They're not that squeaky, so they don't get much grease. That grease can be in the form of time, recognition and if we're honest, respect. It's easier to respect someone who consistently demands it than someone who doesn't. The level of respect you have for a direct report shows up in subtle areas like how quickly you respond to their messages, whether you keep appointments with them and how much energy you put forth to develop them. Like love, respect is an action. By demonstrating respect for Quick-Slow employees, you will inspire their long-term trust and send a message to the rest of the team that you won't take their trust for granted.

Be Trustworthy

Being trustworthy with a high-trust direct report conveys that you believe their trust should be earned. It reinforces that they should feel comfortable extending long term trust to you. It also serves as a coaching opportunity by modeling the behavior they should be looking for before extending trust.

A Word to QUICK-SLOW Professionals

If you're a Quick-Slow professional, this section may have stung a little. No one wants to hear that some may find it difficult to respect them because they're courageous enough to extend trust at the start. You're correct in assessing that the merits of trust can far outweigh its liabilities—especially if you're strong enough to overlook betrayals. Moreover, of the four trust quadrants, only one **(Quick-Quick)** is more effective in terms of **productive efficiency** (the achievement of maximum productivity with minimum effort). To be even more effective, find ways to add probing without diminishing your propensity to trust. For example, the next time you're given a document to approve or contract to sign, read it carefully and make the issuer wait while you read it. This may make you feel non-trusting but remember that trust is the byproduct of probing. You may be surprised how often you find questionable items. Even if you don't, you'll train your co-workers, stakeholders, and vendors that your trust must be earned and if given, should be cherished. The cautionary warning is that if you don't balance trust with probing, negative trust experiences could move you into a trust quadrant that's far less effective.

Earning Trust from Managers in the SLOW-QUICK Trust Quadrant

Managers in the second trust quadrant **(Slow-Quick)** are slow to trust and quick to probe. They're more impacted by the liabilities of trust than its promises. They may have experienced or observed negative outcomes from trusting without sufficient probing. In response, they do more probing than is necessary and less trusting than is warranted. If you work for a Slow-Quick manager, you may feel like you're always under suspicion, despite having proven yourself many times over. The first step in earning their trust is to realize that you have **not** earned their suspicion (unless, of course you have!). This realization is important because when you think you're a suspect, you tend to act like one, which reinforces their low-trust disposition. The next step is to begin earning their trust by being loyal, reliable, and valuable.

Be Loyal

No one appreciates being treated like a suspect, so everyone will have something negative to say about a Slow-Quick manager. Don't join in. I'm reminded of the Progressive insurance commercials about the Parent-Life Coach whose job is to prevent new homeowners from becoming their parents. "We all see it... We all see it!", he says to one of his clients as they gawk at someone with blue hair. Like the Parent-Life Coach in the Progressive commercials, we can all see it when a manager has a low-trust propensity. There's nothing to be gained from joining in on the gossip. There is, however, plenty to lose. Don't reinforce your manager's low-trust propensity by being disloyal. Don't think your disloyalty won't get back to them. People who gossip give off different non-verbal signals than people who don't.

Here are some things you might consider saying when your colleagues invite you to be disloyal.

- "How do you think we should discuss this situation with our manager?"

- "It sounds like you need to speak to her directly."

- "I'd rather talk to him directly than talk about him."

Be Reliable

Being reliable is about guaranteeing the results you commit to. One of the main differences between a seasoned professional and a novice is that seasoned professionals have an excellent track record for delivering the results others rely on them to deliver. This is no accident. It comes from watching things going wrong at the last minute and learning to make provisions to guarantee desired outcomes. One manager considers the job done when they've ordered the equipment. Another, when they've confirmed the equipment has landed on the docks. Another, when they've contacted the site, spoken with the person at the dock who will receive the equipment, and confirmed it will be taken to the appropriate location when it's needed. One manager considers the job done when they've hired a vendor to do it. Another, when they've spoken to the person the vendor assigned to do the job. Another, when they've spoken to the person the vendor assigned, and confirmed they have access to the site. Reliable professionals come through. They appease the concerns of Slow-Quick managers by considering things that can go wrong that their manager hasn't even considered. Because of this practice, even when things do go wrong (you can't catch everything), Slow-Quick managers tend to grant them latitude. They know that if it happened on that person's watch, it could have happened on anyone's watch. They also know that they couldn't possibly hold that person more accountable than that person holds themselves.

Be Valuable

Slow-Quick managers may be slow to trust but they're not slow to discern when one of their direct reports is appreciating in value. Earning relevant certifications, becoming more adept at navigating processes and building valuable alliances are all ways to increase your value. This will help change the focus from whether to trust you to what it might take to keep you happy. One of the most evident ways is to extend more trust and latitude.

Earning Trust from Direct Reports in the SLOW-QUICK Trust Quadrant

Direct reports in the second trust quadrant **(Slow-Quick)** are slow to trust and quick to probe. They're more impacted by the liabilities of trust than its promises. They're very attentive listeners; not because they find your topic engaging, but because they're trying to determine if what you're saying is consistent to what you may have said at an earlier time. They're listening as much for content as for congruency. Slow-Quick direct reports can make you feel like they're trying to catch you in a lie. This is problematic because it can encourage other direct reports to over-analyze the accuracy of your message. As with managers in this trust quadrant, the first step in changing this low-trust dynamic is to realize that you have **not** earned their suspicion. This will keep you from appearing defensive. Your objective should not be to respond to every unfounded suspicion. For every suspicion you address, the Slow-Quick direct report can develop three more. It's far more effective to address the root cause (their low-trust propensity) by being loyal, reliable, and valuable.

Be Loyal

Disloyalty is a non-starter for Slow-Quick direct reports. It reinforces their low-trust disposition by giving it validation. As with Slow-Quick managers, resist the temptation to be disloyal to them by discussing their professional weaknesses with other managers. Slow-Quick direct reports know how they are. They've accepted that their slowness to trust and quickness to probe can be combative and gender ire from managers. Because of this, they can discern if you've disclosed their weaknesses to others by watching for changes in the behavior of other managers toward them. No one can keep your secret better than you can. The best way to ensure disloyalty doesn't get back to your direct reports is to refrain from doing it altogether. Also, consider that by discussing the professional weaknesses of your direct reports with your peers, even for the purpose of seeking input, you may be inadvertently limiting their opportunities to someday work for those managers. Be loyal to your Slow-Quick direct reports and you will do your part in encouraging them to probe for the purpose of extending trust rather than finding fault.

Be Reliable

Few things inspire the trust of Slow-Quick direct reports better than reliability. Employees rely on managers for development opportunities, promotions and "having their back" when the going gets tough. Reliable managers find ways to come through. They appease the concerns of Slow-Quick direct reports by outlining tangible growth opportunities and then delivering on them after they put in the work. They fight for them and think outside of the box to create opportunities for them to grow and progress, even when budgets are limited. Slow-Quick employees will be especially attentive when there are opportunities to "throw them under the bus." Nothing inspires their trust better than when you protect their professional image – especially when they're at fault, by addressing the matter with them privately while publicly supporting them. Your efforts to keep a tight lid on their faux paus will not go unnoticed.

Be Valuable

Slow-Quick direct reports may be slow to trust but they're not slow to discern when they've got a good thing going. It's easy to spot a valuable manager. They focus on employee strengths, avoid micromanaging, develop careers, consider ideas, recognize and reward good work and genuinely appreciate their direct reports. By putting these valuable traits on full display, you can change the focus of the Slow-Quick direct report from whether to trust you to what they can do to remain under your tutelage. One consideration may be to become less combative and less critical about the validity of your messages.

A Word to SLOW-QUICK Professionals

If you're a Slow-Quick professional, you're right to be judicious about extending trust. Trusting the wrong person(s) has led to the downfall of many leaders. Since you invest a good deal of time kicking the tires, consider finding ways to collect a return on your investment. Probing for the sake of probing is like analyzing stocks for the sake of analysis. Your probing should have an aim—to determine where to invest your trust. If you've observed or suffered negative trust experiences in the recent past, this can feel counterintuitive. Withholding trust is the safest path. On the other hand, the kind of productive efficiency you need is only possible in high-trust environments. Trust is not an optional, impotent quality that's nice to have in the workplace. It's a mandatory prerequisite for delivering the quick results needed to survive business disruption. Though you are correct in assessing that it should only be extended when warranted, if you consider it an optional nice-to-have quality, you can concede a permanent, competitive advantage to competitors with high-trust environments. Scary as it may be, in the post-COVID business world and especially in remote work scenarios, trust is more of a prerequisite than a luxury.

Earning Trust from Managers in the SLOW-SLOW Trust Quadrant

Managers in the third trust quadrant **(Slow-Slow)** are slow to trust and slow to probe. Like Slow-Quick managers, they're more impacted by the liabilities of trust than its promises. Unlike Slow-Quick managers, they don't make you feel like a suspect. From their perspective, extending trust is not a consideration. Therefore, they don't bother probing to determine whether you're worthy of trust. Their disposition could be based on experience, observation, philosophy, or a combination of these. As such, the first step in impacting the trust dynamic is to set realistic expectations. You can only play a small role in affecting their propensity to trust. Though the role you play is small, it's not insignificant. You can change a transactional dynamic into a more personal dynamic. Though this is not as significant a shift as moving from low-trust to high-trust, the affability can have a positive impact on morale and therefore productive efficiency. To realize this shift, consider being transparent, productive, and trustful.

Be Transparent

Although a Slow-Slow manager will not be inclined to examine your trustworthiness, nothing prevents you from putting it on full display, nonetheless. Transparency produces a similar outcome to probing—a basis for trust. Don't be discouraged if the Slow-Slow manager does not extend trust in response. Your goal is not to change your manager, but rather to improve your work dynamic. Be transparent about what you're working on, what your goals are, how you're planning to improve and the challenges you face meeting your performance targets. Every manager expects that you'll face challenges meeting your targets. Being transparent about them, presents the opportunity to work together to solve them. This can build rapport and have a positive impact on your work dynamic.

Be Productive

Results can change everything. They can change the mood from fearful to cheerful, pessimistic to hopeful and tense to lighthearted. Becoming more consistent at delivering project outcomes will create a winning environment that feels less transactional and more personal. I'm reminded of the late Jerry Krause, scout and general manager of the 1988 Chicago Bulls. Negatively portrayed in the documentary, *Last Dance*[2], Krause was slow to trust in any one player or coach (even Michael Jordan and Phil Jackson!) and quick to trust in teamwork and in his gift for spotting new talent. The winning culture of the organization overshadowed the clear animosity between he and prominent members of the team. This was touchingly displayed in the documentary, where key members of the team are shown celebrating with Krause. Productivity can change the focus from whether to trust you to what it might take to keep you happy, like giving you more latitude and autonomy.

Be Trustful

Slow-Slow managers have no issues being trustworthy themselves. They're just not fans of extending it. Someone with a keen understanding of the liabilities of trust may be the best steward of it. If your probing justifies it, be trustful of managers in the Slow-Slow trust quadrant. When you trust someone, you disclose mistakes, ask for guidance and trust their intentions. Extending trust increases productive efficiency by 50%, since at least one of the two parties is extending trust. IIt also builds the most compelling case for extending trust back by creating a trust mirror. **Trust mirrors** occur when professionals mirror the trust extended to them.

Earning Trust from Direct Reports in the SLOW-SLOW Trust Quadrant

Direct Reports in the third trust quadrant **(Slow-Slow)** are slow to trust and slow to probe. They're more impacted by the liabilities of trust than its promises. Unlike Slow-Quick direct reports, they don't make you feel like they're trying to catch you in a lie. They're often seasoned professionals that have lost the aspirational spark they may have once had. Their talents may have been overlooked by prior managers or they may have been passed over one too many times. Whatever the reason, they've seen or experienced enough to stop putting their trust in managers. It's important to set realistic expectations about how much you can impact your trust dynamic with them. The decision to trust is theirs to make. What you can do is build the best case for them to extend trust by being transparent, productive, and trustful.

Be Transparent

Slow-Slow direct reports will not probe to determine if you're trustworthy. They're perfectly willing to have a transactional dynamic with you, where your leadership role is reduced to administrative things like approving expense reports and confirming they've completed mandatory training. Send them a signal that there's more to be had under your leadership by being more transparent with them than they might expect. Surprise them. I'm reminded of a director I once reported to who was transparent about the political maneuverings of her colleagues and her counterstrategies. Her authenticity was refreshing. It created a culture of openness, which she used to surface honest reactions and coach the team. Slow-Slow direct reports may not respond by sharing their honest reactions (a sign of trust), but you will have created enough psychological safety for them to do so when they're ready.

Be Productive

As mentioned earlier, results can change everything. Make it your goal to reawaken the aspirational spark Slow-Slow direct reports may have lost. Produce tangible outcomes for them like credible advancement opportunities or the opportunity to take on challenging assignments. Wake them up. Ask questions like, "When is the last time you felt challenged by your job?", "What's the biggest project you've worked on?" and "What leadership challenges do you believe you're ready for?" You may find their answers surprising. Use them as a guide for finding work that will challenge them and dare them to dream again. By producing tangible growth outcomes for Slow-Slow direct reports, you will increase their level of engagement at a minimum and in the best case inspire them to trust you to look out for their interests.

Be Trustful

Like Slow-Slow managers, Slow-Slow direct reports have a keen understanding of the liabilities of trust and may be the best stewards of your trust. If your probing justifies it, demonstrate that you trust Slow-Slow direct reports. Consider trusting them to cover you when you're out of the office. Entrust them with an important project. Trust them to train a new team member. Doing so will increase productive efficiency by 50%, since at least one of the two parties is extending trust. As mentioned earlier, it also builds the most compelling case for extending trust back.

A Word to SLOW-SLOW Professionals

If you're a Slow-Slow professional, you've likely had your position reinforced by experience, observation, and careful thinking. A conclusion reached after due consideration is as immovable as a beam. This section will have reached its aim if it posits fresh ideas for your consideration. In an earlier section, we emphasized that trust is not a luxury, but a perquisite for competing effectively against high-trust teams. This is underscored by the Agile manifesto, which includes the following principle.

Build projects around motivated individuals.
Give them the environment and support they need,
*and **trust** them to get the job done.*

Consider that trust is one of the demands of leadership. It's a risk that leaders can't afford not to take. You can minimize this risk with careful probing, but as you've likely discovered, you can't catch everything. Notwithstanding, if you weigh the promise of trust against its liabilities, the promises will always come out ahead. Consider watching Captain David Marquet's YouTube video, titled *"Turn this ship around"*[3]. It paints a good picture of the productive efficiency that's possible on high-trust teams. Start small. Let the merits of trust motivate you to consider moving into the Slow-Quick quadrant, where you're at least probing to consider the possibility of extending trust. Also, consider extending compartmental trust. For example, if you can't trust someone to deliver an entire project, trust then to deliver a task on a project. Finally, consider that trust is one of the most powerful motivators in business. The worker that has someone's trust will always outperform the worker that has someone's promise of reward or threat of consequence. This is because having someone's trust produces intrinsic motivation, whereas carrots and sticks produce extrinsic motivation.

Earning Trust from Managers in the QUICK-QUICK Trust Quadrant

Managers in the fourth trust quadrant **(Quick-Quick)** are quick to trust and quick to probe. They're more impacted by the promises of trust than its liabilities. Though they may have observed negative outcomes from misappropriated trust, they've tasted the productivity gains of high-trust environments. They seek the best workers and have a good track record for attracting them. They're not the easiest managers to work for because they're quite comfortable holding people accountable and demanding higher levels of performance. If you like to be challenged, want to explore your limits, or simply want to grow as a person, you will likely have a positive experience with Quick-Quick mangers. If you're beholden to the status quo, are comfortable resting on past accomplishments or prefer a more distant, transactional relationship with your manager, you will likely have a negative experience with a Quick-Quick manager. For the best possible outcome, be real, be assertive and be responsive.

Be Real

Quick-Quick managers are as real as they come. They're transparent about who they are and will expect the same from others. This can be a breath of fresh air to some and feel intrusive to others. If you're in the former group, go with the flow. Enjoy the experience and do your best to prolong it. This type of leadership dynamic is rare. If you're in the latter group, bear in mind that being real does not mean you have to be a conformist. Be yourself. Be real about who you are and how you like to operate. If you strike the right balance between being true to yourself and making a genuine effort to embrace a culture of openness and transparency, this manager can help you grow as a leader and as a person.

Be Assertive

Quick-Quick managers tend to be very productive. They set the performance bar high and are willing to invest real effort in helping you meet it. Take an honest assessment of your workload and be prepared to justify pushing back if goals are unrealistic. The value of a high-trust dynamic is that it allows for honest, sometimes uncomfortable interactions. Support opposing viewpoints with data from dashboards, project counts and performance trends. Prepare alternative goals in advance that may be just as impactful to the business but more consistent with operating level agreements. Quick-Quick managers will welcome the engagement and may come back with a counteroffer. Commit yourself to this process. If your manager is insistent on certain terms, negotiate concessions like the following:

- Can we revisit this after a few weeks to see how things are lining up?

- Can we discuss the possibility of offloading work if these projects get too hot?

- Can you pair me up with someone who has done this before until I get a feel for this project type?

Be Responsive

Be willing to be uncomfortable if you're working for a Quick-Quick manager. They will entrust you with more than you think you can handle. In most cases, you'll do better than you expect. In some cases, you'll end up in a coaching session. Responsiveness is the lubricant that will make the work seamless. Be responsive to challenges and responsive to feedback. Be ready to demonstrate your responsiveness by performing better on the next project.

Earning Trust from Direct Reports in the QUICK-QUICK Trust Quadrant

Direct Reports in the fourth trust quadrant **(Quick-Quick)** are quick to trust and quick to probe. They're more impacted by the promises of trust than its liabilities. They're perfect candidates for highly functional, productive teams. They know how fast and efficiently a team can move when trust is present and have higher expectations than most. They will expect you to probe them and discover their trustworthiness and they will expect your trust in return. If you don't return it, you can inadvertently demotivate them. Since they're always probing, they will quickly detect low-trust environments and seek other opportunities when the time is right. To retain these highly functional workers, be real, be assertive and be responsive.

Be Real

Quick-Quick direct reports are as real as they come. They're transparent about how they want to impact the business and how they want to be compensated in return. This can be exciting for some managers and intimidating for others. Despite which group you're in, be as real with them as they are with you. Stay in the driver's seat. Let them know how you prefer to operate, how you approach advancement opportunities and what qualities you seek when you're assigning high-profile projects. Your goal is not to make them happy but to paint a clear picture for them as to how you like to run a team. Even if your style is not their cup of tea, they'll respect your genuineness and will be genuine with you in return. Also, your realness will provide sufficient reason for them to continue to trust you.

Be Assertive

Quick-Quick direct reports can be very assertive. They may openly probe you, not to discover faults or inconsistencies but to confirm that your business decisions are sound and fair. Be sure to match their level of assertiveness. If appropriate, communicate your decisions, beliefs, thoughts, and feelings openly. If the setting or timing is not appropriate, say so and follow up with them at a more appropriate time. This level of assertiveness will encourage them to continue to engage in a high-trust dynamic with you. See Chapter 3 for additional tips on becoming more assertive.

Be Responsive

Do you know what will happen if you don't pick the oranges from your orange tree? The oranges will eventually fall from the tree and over time, the tree will become less productive. The same thing can happen to Quick-Quick direct reports if you're not responsive to their desire to impact the business in significant ways. They will either seek other opportunities or become less productive over time. Sadly, some Slow-Slow employees were once Quick-Quick employees. Do your part in cultivating them and be responsive to their aspirations. Allow their drive to permeate the team and challenge the team (and perhaps yourself!) to be more engaged. These actions will supply ample justification for their sustained trust in you and your leadership.

A Word to QUICK-QUICK Professionals

If you're a Quick-Quick professional, you've tasted the fruit of high-trust dynamics and understand there's no better or more fulfilling way to work. If it hasn't happened already, at some point you'll have a negative experience due to misappropriated trust. As careful an examiner as you may be, you can't catch everything. Some betrayers are impossible to see. The challenge is not to become a Quick-Quick professional, but to remain one after a painful betrayal.

In the words of Sherrilyn Kenyon, author of *Invincible*,

"Everyone suffers at least one bad betrayal in their lifetime. It's what unites us. The trick is not to let it destroy your trust in others ... Don't let them take that from you."

When your trial comes, use it to become a better examiner but resist the urge to let it rob you of the competitive edge that trusting affords you.

Extending Trust (How to Probe)

The liabilities of trust are real and can be quite serious. Some will argue that they outweigh the promises. Nicole Richie said,

---

It's hard to tell who has your back,

from who has it long enough just to stab you in it...

This section is about getting better at determining who to extend trust to. We'll review ten questions you can ask to ensure you're investing trust in the right person.

1. **Are they Consistent?** A trustworthy person is fundamentally the same from audience to audience. They may be polished in one setting and relaxed in another, but their fundamental behavior and character will be consistent. What they say to you matches what others say they said to them. If they change their view, they will own up to the change and won't deny that they ever had such a view.

2. **Are they Compassionate?** A person that lacks compassion will be more comfortable betraying your trust. The heart that lacks compassion or empathy is also capable of lacking remorse.

3. **Are they Humble?** A humble person is less likely to betray than a proud person. They have a more accurate assessment of themselves, tend to be

more reconciled with their status or accomplishments and are less prone to envy, which is the trigger for many betrayals.

4. **Are they Envious?** Envy is discontentment and resentment arising from a longing for someone else's possessions, qualities, or luck. Enviers are careful to hide their resentment from the person they envy but openly disparage them before others. If you notice this propensity in someone, consider that if your fortunes change, their envy could come your way.

5. **Are they Critical?** Some will challenge your *direction* because they feel strongly about a different course. These are keepers. Others will challenge your *leadership* by challenging your direction. The difference can be subtle. Pay attention to your physiological signs. Our emotions and instincts are much quicker to discern threats than our cognitive processes and will trigger physiological indicators, such as sweating and a rising heartbeat. If you notice these indicators every time someone speaks or before they've even gotten to their point, your instincts may be sensing an overly critical spirit.

6. **Are they Relaxed?** Nonverbal signs are difficult to fake. Are routine interactions strained for no apparent reason? Do you exit encounters with this person wondering "what was that about?" Are you asking all the right questions and getting unproductive responses? These are good indications to proceed with caution when it comes to extending trust.

7. **Are they Grateful?** It's professional courtesy to express gratitude for your time or assistance. But if you go above and beyond, you should not only hear the gratitude, but you should also feel it. If you don't, the reasons could range from someone feeling entitled to someone being critical of your leadership. Neither is a good foundation for extending trust.

8. **Are they Trustful?** Trust mirrors work in two ways. If someone has negative feelings toward you, they tend to presume you have negative feelings toward them. They may mask their negative feelings, but their mistrust of you can be a nonverbal reflection of how they anticipate you will respond to them in kind. The opposite is also true. When someone has positive feelings toward you, it can manifest as feelings of trust. This is a good indicator for extending trust.

9. **Do they Gossip?** This is a nonstarter. Gossips are equal opportunity employers. No one's business is immune if its juicy enough.

10. **Do they Exaggerate?** A truthful person tells it like it is and doesn't rely on hyperbole to build their case. Is the process "completely broken" or simply in need of improvements? Was the meeting a "total waste of time" or could it have been ended 10 minutes earlier? Is a project team member "completely unreliable" or did they simply forget an action item? There's a fine line between exaggeration and deceit. If someone is prone to exaggeration, it may be a good idea to probe a bit more before extending trust.

Trust is the lubricant to highly functional teams. According to Patrick Lencioni[4], the absence of it is one of the hallmarks of dysfunctional teams. Asking questions like these before extending trust can help you exploit the promises of trust and minimize its liabilities.

Emotional Intelligence and Trust

Several emotional intelligence traits can have a positive impact on trust. Three traits that are particularly meaningful in remote work situations are Reality Testing, Flexibility and Self-Regard. Following are definitions of each emotional intelligence trait, indicators of high and low effectiveness and steps you can take to improve.

Reality Testing

Trust is one of the most valuable resources in business. To continue realizing its promises, professionals must extend it judiciously. This will minimize negative trust experiences and keep them from slipping into trust quadrants that are slow to trust. The emotional intelligence trait that is most useful in this regard is reality testing. This trait enhances your ability to see people and situations as they really are. From an emotional intelligence standpoint, **reality testing** is the capacity to remain objective by seeing things as they are. It involves recognizing when emotions or personal bias can cause one to be less objective.

The following table includes indicators of high and low effectiveness using this emotional intelligence trait.

Low Effectiveness	High Effectiveness
• Unrealistic • Disconnected • Ignores unpleasant truths	• Objective • Ignores personal bias • Tuned into the environment

Reality testing is as much about accepting unpleasant truths as it is about seeing them. Colleagues that may betray your trust can be likeable or very relatable. These attributes can entice you to be slow to probe and ignore clues that suggest you should withhold trust. As effective as high-trust environments can be, you simply cannot build them in every instance. It's important to be objective when you're vetting trust suitors. Three simple things you can do to become more effective in reality testing, is probe a bit longer, recognize your biases and listen more actively.

1. **Probe a bit longer.** Trust is a sizeable investment. Treat it as you would any investment and "kick the tires" a bit longer. Take your trust suitor out for a test drive if you can. When your goal is to create a high-trust environment, it can be tempting to extend trust after you see the first indicator. There's nothing wrong with waiting for a second or third indicator. The good news is, if your trust suitor is trustworthy those additional indicators will manifest fairly quickly. One of my personal mantras is the truth only gets truer. The same applies to trustworthy people. They only become more trustworthy over time. Conversely, if the second or third supporting indicators never present themselves you might have avoided a painful trust experience.

2. **Recognize your biases.** When it comes to extending trust, the biases to watch for are predispositions to extend trust too quickly, based on how similar you are to the trust suitor and predispositions to extend trust too slowly, based upon how different you are from the trust suitor. The quicker you can recognize your biases, the quicker you can course correct and make objective, fact-based decisions. The best way to recognize your bias is to take an implicit bias test. The Harvard institute publishes an implicit bias test[5] you can take at no cost.

3. **Listen more actively.** Active listening is a technique that enables you to fully concentrate on what others are saying and to understand their complete

message. It encourages dialogue and can surface the supporting facts you need to make a judicious trust decision. In Chapter 5, we will discuss listening techniques in detail. The following infographic provides a quick overview of active listening. You can request a free electronic copy at **https://www. pmplicity.com/contact-us_mspbasics-1.**

ACTIVE LISTENING
Become a Better Listener in 5 Steps

1. Zoom In

Look at the speaker, be aware of their body language, and ignore distractions.

2. Show Some Love

Show that you're listening by nodding, smiling and saying "yes" or "uh-huh" from time to time, to encourage the speaker to continue.

3. Run it Back

Reflect the speaker's words back to them, and ask questions to check that you understand correctly.

4. Wait Your Turn

Allow the speaker to finish their point and make sure you understand it fully before you offer a response or counter argument.

5. Take the Mic

Now that you've respected what the person has to say, chances are pretty good they'll respect what you have to say. When you speak, be open and honest, but be respectful of the speaker's opinion.

6. Repeat

When the other person responds to what you've said, go back to step one and Zoom in again. The more actively you listen, the more actively they will listen!

Flexibility

By getting better at reality testing, you will become more objective by seeing things as they really are. Once you have a firm grasp on the reality of a person or situation, you must then be able to adjust your emotions, thoughts, and behaviors to your new discoveries. By doing so, you will be able to break away from ineffective habitual tendencies and take the best courses of action. From an emotional intelligence standpoint, **flexibility** is the ability to adapt emotions, thoughts and behaviors to unfamiliar, unpredictable, and dynamic circumstances or ideas. It involves the ability to overcome tendencies to be rigid and obstinate when new facts present themselves. The following table includes indicators of high and low effectiveness in this emotional intelligence trait.

Low Effectiveness	High Effectiveness
• Stuck in patterns • Resistant to change • Prefers the status quo • Unresponsive to new information	• Able to adapt to changing circumstances • Open to new ideas and discoveries • Able to release familiar ways of thinking and responding

The worldwide impact of the agile movement provides the strongest validation of the usefulness of flexibility. One of the four values in the Agile Manifesto[6] is "responding to change over following a plan". This value reflects the humility to acknowledge that even the best laid plans are inferior to the ability to respond to change. Following are three tactics you can apply to become more flexible.

1. **Disconnect your ego.** My favorite Colin Powell quote is "Avoid having your ego so close to your position that when your position falls, your ego goes with it." One of the main causes for resistance to change is pride. When we link our ego to a position, person, or plan, it can be difficult to respond to new information because doing so might result in a loss of reputation. Use the wisdom of Colin Powell and disconnect your ego from lofty positions, initial impressions about people and the viability of your plans. It's better to position yourself as an agile professional, who is responsive to change than one who rejects feedback and is not pliable.

2. **Identify the real change trigger.** Sometimes we are inflexible not because we choose to be, but because we haven't identified the supporting habit that keeps us tethered to ineffective outcomes. These supporting habits are what I call **change triggers**. Once we address them meaningfully, change will occur. For example, if you attempt to lose a beer belly by doing a lot of ab exercises (the false change trigger) and don't change your diet (the real change trigger), your beer belly won't change significantly. If you're trying new things and producing the same ineffective outcomes, you may not have identified the real change trigger.

3. **Nurture honest feedback.** New, credible insights can provide compelling reasons in and of themselves to adapt your approach. One way to ensure a steady flow of fresh insights is to nurture honest feedback. If you're quick to extend trust, consider that others may pick up on things you miss. For example, my wife is far better at probing than I am. When I find someone likeable or relatable, I tend to stop probing. My wife keeps her antennae up much longer and on more than one occasion has pointed out compelling, credible indicators that I missed. As much as I dislike having to adjust affable work relationships in response to credible new insights, I resist the urge to challenge her feedback. It has made me a better prober and has led to stronger bonds with colleagues that prove trustworthy. By nurturing honest feedback, you will expand your field of vision and improve the quality of the information you use when deciding whether to extend trust.

Self-Regard

In September of 1940, the Reader's Digest attributed the following quote to Eleanor Roosevelt.

"No one can make you feel inferior without your consent."

Self-regard is the emotional intelligence trait that determines whether you can be made to feel inferior. To showcase its relevance to earning trust, consider which of the following people you would feel more inclined to trust. Base your choice solely on the following descriptions. **Person A** comes off insecure, inadequate, underqualified, and inferior. When they make mistakes, they blame others or deny that they made them to keep from feeling worse about themselves. They often pretend to know more than they do to win the respect of others. **Person B** comes off inwardly strong, secure, self-assured, and confident. They openly acknowledge mistakes and seem comfortable admitting when they don't know something. Based solely on the information provided, most would be quicker to extend trust to Person B than Person A. Self-regard is what distinguishes Person B from Person A. From an emotional intelligence standpoint, **self-regard** is the ability to respect oneself while understanding and accepting both their weaknesses and their strengths. It's often associated with feelings of inner strength and self-confidence. The following table includes indicators of high and low effectiveness in this emotional intelligence trait.

Low Effectiveness	High Effectiveness
• Not confident • Unsure of themselves • Low self-esteem	• Self-Assured • High Self-Esteem • Confident

Low self-regard can be attributed to a range of causes, including disapproving or unsupportive authority figures, traumatic experiences and bullying. Whatever the cause, the person on the receiving end of these experiences must decide whether to build themselves up again or continue tearing themselves down by perpetuating unproductive thought patterns.

Following are three tactics you can use to disrupt negative thought patterns and build self-regard.

1. **Earn an "A+" every day.** Low self-regard doesn't usually manifest all at once. It's often the by-product of years of neglect or abuse. It follows then that building self-regard requires a steady diet of encouragement and triumph. Put yourself in a position to earn an "A+" everyday by determining ahead of time the tasks you can accomplish that would constitute earning a letter grade of "A+". Busy professionals accomplish significant work every day but rarely pause long enough to relish the accomplishment. Disrupt this cycle by acknowledging when you've earned your "A+". Signify your accomplishment

by writing "A+" at the top of your task list. Slowing yourself down to recognize micro-victories like these can have an incremental effect on self-regard.

2. **Stop S-P-I-R-A-Ling.** S.P.I.R.A.L. is an acronym I developed from six well-documented negative thought patterns. It's an easy way to identify and disrupt them before they start eating away at your self-regard.

- **Stop Shrinking.** Shrinking occurs when you shrink the magnitude of your positive accomplishments to make them appear commonplace. For example, if you receive accolades for delivering a project early, don't shrink the magnitude of it by thinking something like "I only finished it so early because it was an easy project."

- **Stop Presuming.** Presuming occurs when you make an unconfirmed negative presumption and use negative outcomes to validate it. For example, if you miss a deadline, don't use it to validate an unfounded negative presumption by thinking something like "I missed my deadline and now everyone will know that I shouldn't have been promoted into his position."

- **Stop Inferring.** Inferring occurs when you reach a negative conclusion with little or no supporting evidence. For example, if your manager leaves an urgent message to get back to her, don't make a negative inference like "She's going to fire me!" or "I must have done something to upset him." Negative inferences like these can make you appear guilty when you're not and cause others to suspect you've done something wrong.

- **Stop Replacing.** Replacing occurs when you replace positive facts with negative feelings. Sometimes you may be doing very well but feeling like a failure. Don't replace positive facts with negative feelings by thinking something like, "Even though I got an excellent review, I feel like a fraud, so I must have all these people fooled."

- **Stop All-Out Thinking.** All-Out thinking occurs when you base your opinion of yourself on whether you are successful in one thing. For example, don't gamble with your self-worth by yielding to all-out thinking like "If I don't close this deal, I'm a complete failure."

- **Stop Lashing.** Lashing occurs when you model the harmful behavior of people who may have abused or bullied you by undervaluing yourself, putting yourself down or engaging in negative self-talk. For example, if something doesn't go your way, don't lash yourself by thinking something like "I don't deserve anything better."

3. **Impress Yourself.** The best way to respect yourself more is to go about earning more of your respect. Make a list of ten things that would really impress you if you did them. This list should include things that you have the capacity to do right now. If you find some of the things on your list intimidating or if you have no idea how to start some of them, then you're on the right track. Now, start making plans to accomplish some of these things. You may find it exhilarating to even make such a list. If so, put your seat belt on because you will enjoy the ride. I did this exercise and am still impressed with some of the things I've attempted or accomplished. My list included running a marathon, writing a book and teaching at a major university. Those are the goals I've achieved. The ones that remain outstanding include completing a triathlon, running a marathon in under 4 hours, and giving a television interview. I won't likely complete every task on my list, but the more I attempt, the richer my life experiences and the better I feel about myself.

Chapter Summary

In this chapter, we defined safe trust as a firm belief in the reliability, truth, ability, or strength of someone, based on sufficient probing. We reviewed four trust quadrants, varying from one another by quickness to trust and quickness to probe. We reviewed tactics for earning trust from managers and direct reports in each trust quadrant and ten questions you should ask before extending trust. We concluded with strategies for increasing emotional intelligence in the areas of Reality Testing, Flexibility and Self-Regard. The tactics recommended in this chapter are empirical. As such, it is entirely possible that tactics prescribed for managers and direct reports in one quadrant could also be effective with managers and direct reports in a different quadrant. Use them as a guide to refine your approach to trust and reinforce your commitment to realizing its promises while mitigating its liabilities. For one additional tactic, see **Appendix H** which includes a customizable communication plan template. As we'll discuss in chapter 5, such a document can enhance communication effectiveness. It can also assist in closing trust gaps by establishing how, when and to whom you will distribute recurring communications. In a post-COVID world that is aggressively embracing remote work, trust is fast becoming a necessity.

References

1. Covey, Stephen. The Speed of Trust. Free Press, 2006.

2. Jason Hehir (Director). (2020). The Last Dance [Documentary Film]. ESPN Films, Netflix, Mandalay Sports Media, Jump 23, NBA Entertainment.

3. Marquet, D. [Inno-Versity]. (2013, October 8). Inno-Versity Presents: "Greatness" by David Marquet [Video]. YouTube. https://www.youtube.com/watch?v=OqmdLcyES_Q&t=18s.

4. Lencioni, Patrick. The Five Dysfunctions of a Team. Jossey-Bass, 2002.

5. The Harvard Institute. "Project Implicit®" implicit.harvard.edu, Harvard, Copyright 2011, https://implicit.harvard.edu/implicit/takeatest.html.

6. Agile Alliance. "Manifesto for Agile Software Development" agilemanifesto.org, Agile Alliance, Copyright 2001, http://agilemanifesto.org/.

5

Communication

"The single, biggest problem in communication is the illusion that it has taken place." When George Bernard Shaw made this observation, there was no internet, social media, email, or teleconferencing platform to proxy face to face communication. Despite this advantage, he referred to effective communication as an illusion. Even with the best of mediums (face to face communication), effective communication is difficult to realize. Shaw's quote highlights that overconfidence in our ability to communicate is at the heart of miscommunication. It keeps us from owning our part in communication failure and worse, from improving. Professionals who are quick to do the hard work of overcoming communication challenges, and slow to credit themselves for having done so have the best chance of turning the illusion of effective communication into reality. They make uncommon choices to guarantee effective communication, often without thinking about it. They visit, make calls and send text messages when others don't. They have an instinct for the precarious nature of communication. They understand that what one listener interprets as gratitude, another can interpret as sarcasm and another, as condescension. This understanding is also evident in the opening quote. The illusion that communication has taken place—that the receiver has correctly interpreted the message the sender intended—causes preventable conflict and re-work. To break through the illusion, we must appreciate how increasingly difficult it is to communicate in a post-COVID world where technology designed to supersede face to face communication is steadily advancing and where the number of businesses and institutions embracing remote work is increasing rapidly. Let's begin our breakthrough by focusing on the interpreted message.

The Interpreted Message

Communication is an act of self-revelation. When we communicate, we always reveal more than we intend. This is because our listeners see more than what we intend to show them. When delivering a message face to face, we may be conscious of our appearance, word choice, timing, and relationship with the listener among other things. Our listeners will also consider these things, but they'll factor in more data. They'll watch what we do with our hands, listen to changes in our volume, pitch or rate of speech and spend a good deal of time reading our eyes. If they know us well, they'll look for patterns in our behavior that we may not be aware of. They'll recall that we always scratch our ears when we're lying or repeat a question when we don't want to answer it. As a result, their interpretation of our message will likely be a more accurate depiction of our intent than our own. This is scary stuff! It's easier to believe we have more control over the messages we send. But the truth is, we only control whether to communicate or not communicate—that is, whether to reveal ourselves or not reveal ourselves. The interpretation is in the hands of the listeners. Herein lies our greatest challenge and perhaps, our greatest opportunity to improve communication effectiveness. If we follow the lead of our listeners and consider both the verbal and non-verbal aspects of the messages we convey, we can significantly improve communication effectiveness.

Albert Mehrabian, UCLA Professor Emeritus is known for his study[1] on the relative importance of verbal and nonverbal messages. He concluded that when a listener interprets a mixed message, they will assign greater weight to the non-verbal aspects of the message than to the verbal. They'll assign a 7% weighting to the words used to express the message, 38% to vocal tones and 55% to facial expressions. For example, if you had lunch with a friend who recently underwent a breakup and they asserted, "I'm actually glad we broke up", would you believe them? Per Mehrabian's study, that would depend on how well their words aligned with their non-verbal signals. If their vocal tone sounded sad and their face looked sad, you would not believe them. You would be 7% convinced by their words, but 93% unconvinced by their non-verbal signals (38% sad vocal tones + 55% sad facial expression). Their non-verbal cues will carry more weight. If ten people observed the conversation, they would likely all agree with you.

Now, suppose your friend sounded happy when they said these words, but their eyes looked sad. Would you believe them then? Let's do the math. You'd be 7% convinced by their words, 38% convinced by their vocal tones and 55% unconvinced by their sad facial expression. Per Mehrabian's study, you would not believe them because sad eyes are more convincing than happy words, said in a happy tone. If ten people observed this interaction, the majority would likely agree with you.

Now, suppose you were speaking to your friend by phone and couldn't see their face. Would you believe them then? Without access to the facial information that might lead you to a different conclusion, you would only be partially convinced. To interpret the message, you would use whatever non-verbal cues you could discern to make up the remaining 55%. This might include the timing of their words, the timing of the call, how many times you've had the same conversation, the length of the conversation and so forth. And here's where it gets interesting. If ten people heard the same phone conversation, they might all interpret the message differently. It's conceivable that half the listeners would believe your friend and half wouldn't. When we supersede face to face communication with telecommunication, we remove 55% of the data required to interpret a message, thereby introducing a probability for error of up to 55%. The same holds true if you removed access to vocal information and were communicating by text only. You'd only have 7% of the data required to correctly interpret the message. Your interpretation would be subject to a margin of error of up to 93%; not because you're not perceptive but because you're working with limited information. Mehrabian's study shines a bright light on the fact that our reliance on new media to communicate is both a help and a hinderance. New media is helpful because it makes communication easy and ubiquitous. It enables global collaboration that might be otherwise impossible. On the other hand, it hinders our ability to correctly interpret messages by removing up to 93% of the information we need to do so. Therefore, to communicate effectively when working remotely, we must get better at non-verbal communication and learn to communicate simply. Simplification is the process of making something easier to do or understand. The five tactics that follow are meant to do just that.

How to Simplify your Message

To simplify your message, you must **think** clearly. Einstein said, "If you can't explain it simply, you don't understand it well enough." Understanding what you feel and what you intend to say is essential if you want to simplify your message. If you can't express your message simply, you don't understand your feelings and intentions well enough. The next step is just as important. You must **listen**. Effective listening increases your chances of interpreting messages correctly. You must improve your ability to perceive verbal and non-verbal cues. You must also work to understand what these cues mean in cultures different from your own. The next step is to **care**. Caring establishes trust, which makes effective communication easy and attainable. Once you've established a solid foundation of clear thinking, perceptive listening, and critical caring, you should consider your communication goals and your recipient to **tailor** your message. Tailoring is a thoughtful process that involves styling your message to maximize receptivity and readability. The final step is to carefully **package** your message by selecting the best medium. Media can enhance your message if you use it thoughtfully. Not only can it get your message heard, but it can also be a part of the message. By getting better at thinking, listening, caring, tailoring, and packaging, you can attain the elusive goal of ensuring that the interpreted message matches your intended message.

Think

How often does something affect your ability to think clearly at work? I ask this question whenever I deliver leadership training. When I suggest twice a week, about 30% of the audience raises their hands. I get 60% of the audience when I suggest daily. I get almost 100% when I suggest hourly. The workplace can be an emotional setting. Any number of things can stir your emotions in a typical workday. A colleague can get selected for a project or promotion you were hoping for. A peer can ask for something in a way that sounds more like a command than a request. Your manger can have a conversation with you that you're not sure is a reprimand or harmless clarification of policy. Incidents like these can trigger emotions that can impair your ability to think clearly. The problem is—we go on communicating anyway, often unaware of our impaired state. When we do, communication disconnects follow. I'm reminded of a communication faux pas I narrowly escaped. It began when my manager sent a team announcement that we would all be required to attend Microsoft Project training. I had already established a reputation on the team as a Microsoft Project expert and several of my colleagues regularly asked me questions about the software. My manager even knew that I was teaching a Microsoft Project course at UCLA Extension. I felt emotions ranging from disappointment to resentment for not being asked to contribute to the training. To make matters worse, I didn't recognize my emotions; partly because I didn't want to feel them in the first place. I wanted to be OK with my manager's choice because this was more appealing to my ego. Not caring was a much more desirable response than being hurt that she didn't consider me. I therefore went forth pretending not to be hurt. This continued right up to the training session. About ten minutes into the session, I raised my virtual hand to ask a question. Luckily, the trainer took a while to get to my question. It gave me time to clarify my feelings and intent. I had the following conversation with myself. *"Jerry, you really don't have a question, do you? You're hurt that your boss didn't acknowledge your expertise, and you're intending to challenge the trainer over a minor technical oversight to appease your ego. Your issue is with your manager, not the trainer"*. When the trainer got around to my question, I told him that he'd already addressed it. By retracting, I avoided a communication faux pas. I was able to think clearly enough to clarify my emotions (hurt feelings) and my intent (to undermine the instructor). By thinking clearly, and sorting out my emotions, I was able to make the right communication decision to put my virtual hand down and keep my mouth shut. If I hadn't, I would have lost rapport with the trainer, as he would have sensed my ire through my undermining question and non-verbal cues. I would have also lost points in professionalism with my colleagues, as they would have confirmed that my ego was bruised (which they likely already suspected) and deemed me petty for attacking the trainer. Ironically, my ego was the winner that day because by keeping silent, I appeared not to care. The point of this story is that to even have a shot at effective communication, we must do two things:

1. Clarify emotions.

2. Clarify intentions.

These are the most important things to get right, especially when you're communicating virtually. Any errors at this stage will propagate through the entire communication exchange. We'll begin with clarifying emotions.

Clarifying Your Emotions

Emotional clarity is a product of emotional intelligence, specifically self-awareness. Every emotional intelligence model uses self-awareness as a foundation for other concepts, such as self-expression and interpersonal relationships. **Emotional self-awareness** is the ability to recognize how you're feeling, why you're feeling that way and the impact your thoughts and feelings have on yourself and others. In the story I relayed earlier, this is what kicked in at the last minute and kept me from attempting to undermine my trainer.

We emote much faster than we can process our emotions. This is a good thing because our emotions are much more intelligent than we are. I find it ironic therefore, that we use the term emotional intelligence. Emotions are already intelligent. For example, we can accurately sense danger and feel fear much quicker than we can articulate why we're afraid. What we sense in a few seconds can take hours, days or even months to process and explain. Therefore, Einstein's quote cited earlier is quite relevant. "If you can't explain it simply, you don't understand it well enough." If you can't explain your emotions simply, you don't understand them well enough. The same applies to intent.

As was the case in my scenario, emotions and intent often have a causal relationship. I was intending to undermine the trainer because of my displaced emotions of disappointment and resentment toward my manager. There isn't always a causal relationship between emotion and intent but when strong feelings are involved it's more prevalent. In this case, the communicator must work twice as hard to clarify emotions.

Here are four recommendations:

1. Stop judging your emotions

2. Acknowledge your physical symptoms

3. Accept what's causing your feelings

4. Expand your emotional vocabulary

Stop Judging Your Emotions

All emotions contain valuable information, even the unpopular ones like jealousy, envy, or shame. For example, jealousy doesn't always stem from insecurity. It stems from a credible sense that something is off. At a minimum, it signals that a good conversation is in order. To envy is to desire to have a quality, possession or other desirable attribute belonging to someone else. This information is valuable for anyone seeking to better themselves. For example, envying a co-worker's position could signal a need to better yourself professionally. Another unpopular emotion is shame, which is a painful feeling of humiliation caused by the consciousness of wrong or foolish behavior. This is a useful emotion, because if embraced, it can keep you from repeating the same mistakes. Denying the existence of emotions you're not proud of is like denying that the check engine light is on in your car. Don't judge or deny your feelings before you can harness the information contained within them to understand yourself and communicate better.

Acknowledge Your Physical Symptoms

If you have trouble clarifying your emotions, there's hope. We're all equipped with a fallback mechanism—the physical symptoms that accompany our emotions. When you're being swindled or insulted or attacked, your body will let you know through physical changes. You may begin to sweat, or maybe your heart will beat faster. These physiological indicators are telling you something important. Hans Selye, who originated and defined the word stress, describes this phenomenon as the Alarm stage of his General Adaptation Syndrome (GAS) model[2]. The Alarm stage is triggered by the perception of a stressor. During this stage, the body will experience an increase in heartbeat, blood flow, blood pressure, oxygen demand and blood sugar levels. This will be accompanied by tensing muscles, sweating, dilating pupils and slower digestion. These physical symptoms may be your first clue that something is off in your communication exchange. If you train yourself to acknowledge these symptoms, you'll have an opportunity to process and clarify your emotions.

Accept What's Causing Your Feelings

If you get good at clarifying your emotions, you'll have come a long way but there's another important and often difficult step. You'll have to accept what's causing your feelings. It's one thing to acknowledge that you envy your colleague. It's quite another to accept that you may be feeling that way because they're outperforming you. Accepting unpleasant truths is vital to the communication exchange because it keeps you on topic and sets the stage for the next step in the process, which is to clarify your intent. If you have trouble accepting unpleasant truths, consider that the time you spend in denial could be spent creating better truths. For example, the sooner you accept that you're being outperformed, the quicker you can step up your game and develop a strategy to excel in an area that plays to your strengths.

Expand your Emotional Vocabulary

When you stop judging your emotions before you can assess them, start acknowledging your physical symptoms and stop denying what's causing your feelings, you can do the interesting work of naming your emotions. The ability to name your emotion(s) is the clearest indicator that you understand them. An exhaustive emotional vocabulary will serve you well in this regard. Several theories have been put forth to identify the different types of emotions. Some suggest there are eight basic emotions, some many more. The following list[3] of 60 emotions was extracted from theories proffered by a recent UC Berkely study, Silvan Tomkin, Robert Plutchik and Aristotle. This list is not exhaustive, but it's a good start.

60 EMOTIONS			
Admiration	Contempt	Gloomy	Reflective
Adoration	Dejected	Guilty	Relieved
Affirmed	Despair	Happy	Romantic
Amused	Determined	Hateful	Sadness
Anger	Devoted	Horrified	Satisfied
Anticipation	Discouraged	Interested	Self-hostility
Anxiety	Disdain	Inspired	Shameful
Appreciation	Disgust	Joy	Shyness
Awe	Empathetic	Kind	Sulky
Awkwardness	Entranced	Loving	Sullen
Boredom	Envious	Lustful	Surprised
Calm	Excited	Modest	Sympathetic
Celebratory	Fearful	Nostalgic	Triumphant
Cheerful	Flustered	Pensive	Trustful
Confused	Friendly	Proud	Vengeful

Use this list to expand your emotional vocabulary and trigger your own thoughts to clarify your emotion(s) by putting a name to them. For example, if a co-worker gets promoted ahead of you, you might be discouraged, dejected, or simply surprised. Discerning between these emotions can help you better understand yourself and devise the best communication path.

Clarifying Your Intentions

Intentions are often driven by undetected and therefore unmanaged emotions. This causal relationship is at the root of many communication disconnects. Once you've clarified and accepted what you're feeling and why you're feeling that way, you'll be in the best state to clarify and assess your intentions. Clarifying intentions amidst strong emotions requires clear thinking. As mentioned earlier, we emote faster than we can process our emotions. Therefore, clarifying intent can be more difficult than it appears. William Zinsser, the best-selling author of "On Writing Well"[4] wrote, "thinking clearly is a conscious act that writers must force on themselves." Here are two recommendations to help you think clearly enough to clarify your intentions when sending a message:

1. Give yourself an intermission.

2. Give yourself an interview.

Give Yourself an Intermission

To get better at clarifying your intent, you must create a conscious intermission between your emotions and your intentions. Use it to challenge your intentions. If you do this right, sometimes you'll conclude that the best communication is no communication at all. Other times you may conclude it's time to pick up the phone, gracefully end the exchange or postpone it to give yourself time to think. In the scenario I shared earlier, this intermission resulted in lowering my virtual hand and changing my message. Bear in mind that the communication cycle can be very unforgiving. Starting an ill-advised communication exchange is like accidentally boarding an express train in Chicago. These trains go straight to the end point and skip all stops in between. Though they are clearly marked as express trains, distracted passengers often board them by mistake. Once they do, they must stay on until the train reaches its posted destination. Few things are as time-consuming and emotionally draining as getting stuck in a communication exchange that has lost its way. A two-minute intermission can save you two hours of frustration.

Give Yourself an Interview

No one can clarify your intent better than you can. Advisors can help, but only by asking questions. Therefore, the best thing you can do to clarify your intentions is to interview yourself. Here's a good list questions to get you started.

- Has this communication exchange shifted my emotional state?
- If so, what caused the shift?
- Have I interpreted the other party's message correctly?
- Should I postpone this exchange until I've had time to process my emotions?
- What was my original intent when this exchange started?
- Did my intent change at any point?
- Did I develop any new, unhealthy intentions as the exchange progressed?
- What outcome do I want from this exchange?
- What outcome do I want for the other party in this exchange?
- Are these outcomes still achievable?
- If so, what's the best way to achieve these outcomes at this point?
- Am I using the most effective medium for the type of exchange we're having?
- Would it be best if I sent no response at all?
- Would someone else be better suited to respond to this message?

Taking the time to answer questions like these will keep you on topic and guarantee the most productive outcome possible.

Listen

The Roget Thesaurus defines listening as "to perceive by ear". This definition captures the objective of listening, which is to accurately interpret messages. Professionals spend up to 63% of their day listening. This finding, published in Owen Hargie's *Skilled Interpersonal Communication*[5], supports that the most direct way to improve worker productivity is to improve listening skills. Notwithstanding, few professionals take courses on effective listening. It follows then that communication challenges are one of the most common causes of project failure. Poor listening leads to inaccurate interpretations, which we wholly rely on to craft responses. Therefore, any improvement in the way we listen will directly improve the way we communicate. To improve listening, you must learn to:

1. Improve Non-Verbal Awareness

2. Zoom In

3. Zoom Out

Improve Non-Verbal Awareness

The Mehrabian study referenced earlier established that non-verbal cues are far more useful than words when listening to and interpreting messages. Why? Because they're harder to fake. If you get excited, your pupils will dilate, and a careful observer will pick up on your excitement. That's why the best poker players in the world wear shades. Non-verbal signals always reveal more than we intend to. Therefore, one of the best ways to improve the non-verbal messages you send is to be sincere. Your non-verbal signals will support your message and bolster your credibility. Unfortunately, sincerity alone won't prevent misunderstandings. You'll also need to improve your ability to monitor and read non-verbal signals.

Non-verbal signals are studied across five areas.

1. **Kinesics (Body Language)** — the study of non-verbal messages sent through movement of the hands, arms, body, face, and eyes.

2. **Haptics (Touch Language)** — the study of non-verbal messages sent through touch.

3. **Vocalics (Tonal Language)** — the study of non-verbal messages sent through vocal qualities that accompany verbal messages, such as tone of voice, volume, rate of speech and verbal fillers like "uhm" and "uh".

4. **Proxemics (Proximity Language)** — the study of non-verbal messages sent through the amount of physical distance established between persons.

5. **Chronemics (Timing Language)** — the study of non-verbal messages related to time.

In remote environments, the relevant areas of study are kinesics, vocalics and chronemics. Therefore, we'll focus our tactics on improving body language, tonal language, and timing language.

Improving Body Language

Kinesics is the study of non-verbal messages sent through movement of the hands, arms, body, face, and eyes. When people refer to reading "body language", they're talking about Kinesics. When you communicate only by audio and text, this is the information you lose. It's always there, but you can't read it because of your choice of media. For this reason, videoconferencing generally results in fewer communication disconnects than audioconferencing alone.

Here are suggestions for **sending** body language.

1. **Turn on the cameras.** You can't see body language unless you enable your video. It's easier to misinterpret a person's tone if you can't see their face. Enabling video during meetings is not only more personable, but it can also improve the way we interpret messages.
2. **Be animated.** If speaking by audio only, stand up or make gestures as if your listener were standing in front of you. These animations will make your words sound more engaging.
3. **Don't advertise nervousness.** Nervous people make other people nervous. If you're nervous during a video meeting, do something deliberate with your hands, like interlocking your fingers. This will keep you from advertising that you're nervous.
4. **Eliminate distractions.** Remove things from your view that can attract your eyes – like clocks and televisions. Shifting your eyes from place to place can make your listener think you're lying or not paying attention.
5. **Smile.** During tense interactions, start the conversation with a smile. Smiles are contagious and can set a pleasant tone for an otherwise unpleasant interaction.
6. **Study your listener's culture.** Study the culture of your listener. What you do with your hands, face, and eyes and what you wear can be interpreted in surprising ways by cultures different from your own. Richard Gesteland's *Cross-Cultural Business Behavior*[6] gives excellent guidance on factoring in cross-cultural differences in communication.

Like most activities, communication is a total body experience. For instance, we don't just run with our legs. The entire body gets involved in ways we don't realize until afterwards, when aches, pains and injuries show up in surprising places. Similarly, we don't just communicate with our mouths. For example, when the answer to a question is "no" and someone means to lie and say "yes", their head may instinctively nod "no" while their mouth is saying "yes". The key to interpreting body language is to pay attention.

Here are suggestions for **interpreting** body language.

1. **Open palms or crossed arms.** When we're being open and truthful, we naturally open our palms. Conversely, when we're closed or defensive, we generally cross our arms.
2. **Leaning forward or backward.** When we're interested, we lean forward, whereas leaning back can show informality or indifference.
3. **Chin, thumb, and index finger.** When we're evaluating something that doesn't quite add up, we tend to support the chin with the thumb while extending the index finger toward the eye or temple.
4. **Stroking the chin.** When we're trying to make a decision, we tend to stroke the chin.
5. **Culture.** Study the culture of your listener. Per Richard Jones's Communication in the Real World[7], the biggest cultural differences in nonverbal communication occur within the categories of eye contact, touch, and personal space.

Improving your Tonal Language

Vocalics is the study of non-verbal messages sent through vocal qualities that accompany verbal messages, such as tone of voice, volume, rate of speech and verbal fillers. As such, vocalics can be observed through face to face, video, and phone communications. Since vocalics includes tone of voice, it can also be observed through written messages, such as text and email correspondence. Here are some suggestions for **sending** tonal language.

1. **Always greet.** A greeting or the lack thereof sends a message and sets a tone. Consider the difference in tone between the following messages.
   - "Can you send over the reports?"
   - "Hi Zoe. Can you send over the reports?"

Most would prefer to receive the second message over the first. It not only acknowledges Zoe's person, but it also says "hello" before making a request. It prioritizes the person over the transaction. The first message can be interpreted as anger, condescension, rudeness, or a lack of respect. If this is not your intent, consider starting your message with a greeting. This is especially important if you're sending a written message.

2. **Brevity.** Short messages can be easily misinterpreted. While they can convey a positive message, like you're respectful of someone's time, they can also convey that you're being curt or even rude. If you're in a rush and need to send a short message, give a reason for your brevity, in a friendly tone. Here's an example.

   ▪ Hi Zoe. Sorry to press, but I'm trying to make a 4PM deadline. Can you send over the report?

3. **Credible emojis** 😊😊😐😣**.** Emojis can work wonders in terms of conveying intent when sending a message. They convey that you're aware your tone could be misinterpreted and want to clarify the tone you're aiming for. Never dilute these powerful aids by sending an emoji that is not consistent with your intent. Remember, your listeners always hear (or read) more than you want them to. Control your message by sending emoji's that truly reflect your intent.

4. **Minimize verbal fillers.** The less you say "umm" and "uh", the more credible you'll appear and the more persuasive you'll be. The more prepared you are, the less you'll use verbal fillers like these. Slowing down your rate of speech also helps. It gives you time to formulate your thoughts. Finally, try saying "hmm" instead or "Let me think about that for a second". "Hmm" is still a verbal filler but it conveys that you're reflecting rather than scrambling to find your words.

5. **Use vocal variety.** The more vocal variety you use, the more interesting you'll be and the more attentive your listener will be. Vary your rate of speech, volume, and tone of voice to keep your listeners engaged.

Here are suggestions for **interpreting** tonal language.

1. **Use multiple indicators.** To increase your chances of correctly interpreting the tone of a message, look for more than one indicator. The more indicators, the better. For example, if you think someone's message is snarky, refrain from engaging your feelings until you have more data. Does their timing support this interpretation? Does the context support a snarky response? Does their body language suggest it? Do your best to reserve judgement until you have multiple supporting indicators.

2. **Delay your emotional response.** The quickest way to derail a communication exchange is to engage your feelings too quickly. Practice delaying your emotional response until you are 100% sure of the sender's intent. Aristotle said "Anyone can become angry. That is easy. But to be angry with the right person and to the right degree, and at the right time and for the right purpose, and in the right way. That is not within everybody's power and is not easy." The best way to gain this power is to practice delaying your emotional response until you have <u>all</u> the supporting evidence for your interpretation of the other person's tone. In my experience, 50% of the time that supporting evidence will never present itself.

3. **Focus primarily on intent.** Be more concerned with intent than content. Allow people to make mistakes in terms of word choice and timing. Focus more on what they're trying to say than how well they're saying it. This will establish an easy-going dynamic that will be returned to you when you make a communication faux pas yourself.

Improving your Timing Language

Chronemics is the study of non-verbal messages related to time. Timing language (the messages you send and interpret relating to time) can be observed across all mediums. Timing is often overlooked as a form of communication. Many professionals convey messages by their timing that they don't realize until after the message has been interpreted and acted upon. The most effective step you can take to improve your non-verbal awareness of timing language is to be aware of its existence and impact on communications. Analyze both of the following scenarios and consider the messages that were sent through the language of timing.

SCENARIO 1— Instant messages between co-workers.

SCENARIO 1— Analysis.

While we can't identify the specific message that Kevin is conveying through his timing language, some of the possible interpretations can reflect negatively upon his professional image. Here are some possible interpretations.

- Kevin is not being forthright about his real motive for contacting Suzanne.

- Kevin didn't want to admit that he was following up again with Suzanne, even though he had followed up the day before.

- Kevin is not a straight-forward, truthful person.

- Kevin doesn't respect Suzanne's time.

- Kevin doesn't trust Suzanne to follow through on her commitment.

- Kevin was simply distracted.

SCENARIO 2 - Instant messages between co-workers.

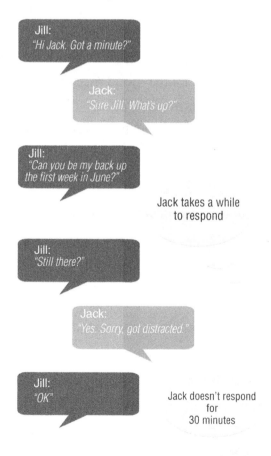

SCENARIO 2 — Analysis.

As with any message related to timing, one cannot interpret it with specificity. Notwithstanding, it appears to Jill that Jack doesn't want to be her backup. This will not bode well for establishing good rapport. It's not necessary that Jack becomes Suzanne's backup to maintain good rapport. It is necessary though, that he gives her a straight answer. By "ghosting", he's allowed for the following possible interpretations, some of which can reflect negatively on Jack's professional image.

- Jack was stalling, hoping that Suzanne would ask someone else.

- Jack didn't want to admit that he didn't want to be Jill's backup.

- Jack wanted to appear more helpful than he is by not explicitly saying no.

- Jack uses the excuse of being "super busy" to hide the fact that he's not willing to help out his teammate.

- Jack wants to maintain good rapport by using deception rather than by being truthful and direct.

- Jack was simply busy and didn't have time to check his schedule.

Did you notice that each scenario included at least one interpretation that was perfectly justifiable? While lapses in time, awkward silences and "pregnant pauses" can have reasonable explanations, these scenarios highlight the need to be aware of the messages we can send through timing.

Zoom In

There's no such thing as undivided attention. The maximum speech rate is 175 words per minute. The maximum rate at which we can process words is 800 words per minute. What do you think we do with all that extra processing capacity? We process other things, like when we're going to file our taxes, what we're going to make for dinner and which task we'd be working on if we weren't in this communication exchange. By the time we return to the conversation, there's a good chance we missed something. Zooming in is about making better use of that excess mental capacity. To do so, you'll need to start practicing the three **Rs** and stop practicing the three **Fs**.

1. **Practice the three Rs.** Put your excess mental capacity to use by **repeating** what the speaker says. This is an active listening tactic that gives the speaker positive affirmation that you're listening. Try repeating the last few words someone says at random points in the conversation. Nothing confirms their message is getting through better than hearing their words repeated back to them. For example, if the speaker says "I'm not trying to be pushy. I just want a fair deal". If you respond "Ok. So, you want a fair deal". The speaker will appreciate your engagement because they know their message is getting through. You could also try **rephrasing** the speaker's message. This will enable them to tweak your understanding if you get it wrong. We'll come back to this point later, as it's helpful for both zooming in and zooming out. Finally, try **restructuring** the speaker's message to make it easier to process. The more organized the speaker's thoughts are and the more emotionally intelligent they are, the less you'll need to do this. The less organized their thoughts are and the less emotionally intelligent, the more you'll need to be an active participant in helping both you and the speaker understand their message. This is especially helpful when the speaker is conveying an emotional message. As mentioned earlier, we emote faster than we can process our feelings. Therefore, listening to an emotional message is less about receiving a message and more about collaborating with the speaker to discover together what the message is. For example, if a colleague confides in you about a difficult conversation they had with their manager, you could help summarize their points, distinguish between supporting examples and main ideas, or offer credible interpretations of their supporting examples. These are all ways to

restructure their message to make it easier to process. As you can see, there are several productive ways to utilize your excess mental capacity. Use it to repeat, rephrase and restructure the speaker's message.

2. **Stop practicing the three Fs.** Most listeners respond to the 625 words per minute gap between the spoken word and the processed word by **floating** away. They process other unrelated thoughts with their spare mental capacity. This seems a good use of time because most professional are juggling many things simultaneously. The downside is, you'll run the risk of mismanaging the current communication exchange and having to make time for it again. By refraining from floating away, you can ensure the matter gets fully addressed the first time. Unlike listeners who float away, some listeners are so focused on the present communication exchange that they devote the time they're not speaking to **formulating** their counter response. This is especially true during heated exchanges. By doing so, they miss important nonverbal messages. The time spent formulating would have been better spent identifying and addressing root causes. For example, a conversation that appears to be about when you'll be free to discuss a matter with your boss may really be about whether you respect her authority enough to *make* time for it. The final **F** to refrain from is embarrassing for most of us to admit. When we float away from the communication exchange to process unrelated matters or spend time formulating instead of listening, we often return to the communication exchange only to find that we haven't a clue what the speaker is talking about. Therefore, we start **faking** it. We scramble for clues and try to look as engaged as possible. The good news is everybody does it. The bad news is no one wants it done to them. If you find yourself in this scenario, you'll need to consider your relationship with the speaker to plot your way forward. If you have a strong relationship, you can be a bit more honest and direct. You can say something like, "I'm sorry, I got distracted. Can you repeat that?" They'll be disappointed that you floated away, but they'd be more disappointed if they caught you faking it. If you don't have a strong enough rapport with the speaker to recover from a mistake like this, it's still in your best interest to avoid faking it and risking credibility loss. Consider asking a clarifying question. If you can't come up with one, it's better to take a risk being honest about having gotten distracted than taking a risk losing credibility for trying

to fake it. Better still, practice the three Rs and avoid situations like this altogether.

Zoom Out

The final step to improve your listening skills when working remotely is to zoom out. Zooming out involves listening for themes and ideas to summarize the small and varied details. Three ways to do this is to challenge your preexisting ideas, the message itself and your interpretation.

1. **Challenge Preexisting Ideas.** One of the things that makes communication efficient is the natural mental process of grouping ideas into patterns or schemata that we can use to craft responses. We also do this with people. For example, when speaking with someone from a different generation, it's natural to use preexisting generalizations to guide your responses. The more accurate your generalizations, and the more sensitivity you show in response, the more effective the communication exchange will be. Therefore, keep your ideas about the person you're communicating with and the topic you're discussing current by being curious and adaptive. Curiosity and adaptivity will keep you from responding to preexisting ideas and allow you to respond to the person in front of you.

2. **Challenge the Message.** This may seem counterproductive, but it's the strongest indicator of engagement. Challenging the message shouldn't be a combative exercise, but a clarifying one. The message you receive from the sender should be credible, complete, and useful. If it's not, challenge it in a sensitive, effective way. For example, if a commitment date does not appear credible, ask "How do you plan to make that date, given the deadline is two weeks away?" If a message does not appear complete, ask "Are there any other factors you can share that support this position?" If a message does not appear useful, ask "How can this information help us solve the problem?" The key to asking these questions without appearing snide or sarcastic is to be genuinely curious. If you think the other party will take your challenge questions the wrong way, couch them in sensitive language. For example, "I'm sorry. But I don't see how this information can help us solve the problem. Can you explain?"

3. **Challenge your Interpretation.** The best way to challenge your interpretation of the sender's message is to **rephase** it. Be responsive to their corrections and then try again. Keep rephrasing until they confirm you've got it right. This is where keeping your emotions in check will come in handy. Emotions should always be kept at bay until you are 100% certain you have interpreted the sender's message correctly. As you go through this process, look for tells that confirm you're on the right track. For example, when you get it right, the speaker's eyes may light up, or their volume may increase. They may become more animated or simply smile. These are all indicators that you've interpreted their message correctly.

Care

To **care** is to have a strong liking for someone, regard them as important or look out for their interests. Caring establishes a basis for trust, which greatly enhances the communication process. For example, someone you believe has your best interest at heart can say "Don't forget we have a team meeting today", and you'll interpret it as a helpful reminder. Someone you don't trust has your best interest at heart can say the same thing and you may interpret it as an insinuation that you're not on top of things. Following are additional statements that could be interpreted differently, based upon whether you believe the communicator cares about you.

Question	Interpretation Based on CARE	Interpretation Based on NO CARE
Did you complete your action item?	They're trying to determine if my action item is complete.	They're hoping I didn't complete my action item so they can discredit me.
Do you know if we're meeting as a team today?	They're trying to determine if we're meeting as a team today.	They're testing me to see if I know whether there's a meeting today so they can disparage me with the boss.
What did you think about the townhall meeting today?	They want to know what I thought about the townhall meeting today.	They want to get me to speak negatively about the leadership team, so they can disparage me.

Question	Interpretation Based on CARE	Interpretation Based on NO CARE
How long will you be on vacation?	They want to know how long I will be on vacation.	They're going to complain to the boss about how long I will be on vacation.
Are you coming to the Happy Hour event?	They want to know if I'm coming to the Happy Hour event.	They're planning something. I better not drink too much.

Did you notice that in every case, the interpretation based on care was a word for word match with the sender's message? This is how easy communication exchanges can be when you care for the listener and thereby, establish a foundation of trust. When your listener doesn't trust you, the communication process breaks down before it even begins. Recall that communication is effective when the receiver's interpretation matches the sender's intent. When you care for the person you're communicating with, there's a good chance they trust your intentions. Effective communication is not guaranteed in this scenario, but it is possible. When you don't care for the person you're communicating with, there's a good chance they don't trust your intentions, rendering effective communication impossible. Therefore, establish a foundation of care with your listener. You have three opportunities, based on the definitions offered earlier. You can like the person you're communicating with, regard them as important or simply look out for their interests.

1. **Like the person you're speaking to.** When people like each other, they tend to trust one another, and they communicate easier. This type of affinity won't happen naturally in every case, but if you look hard enough (sometimes very hard!) you can find something you appreciate about the person you're communicating with. Focus on those attributes and the nonverbal messages you send will be more positive. Also, make it a point to comment on something they've expressed an interested in. For example, if they showcase sports memorabilia, try asking "How do you think your team will do this year?" Be careful using this tactic. You might just end up liking each other!

2. **Regard the person you're speaking to as important.** You can't establish a rapport with everyone, but you can regard everyone as important. Regard can cover a lot of ground in terms of effective communication. At a minimum, it proactively addresses one of the main causes of communication failure— the perception that the other party doesn't respect you. Be deliberate in this area. Let your listener know that you respect their time and their person. One quick way to do this is to organize your message and deliver it as succinctly as possible. Another is to confirm whether someone has time to process your request rather than assuming they do. Yet another is to follow through on commitments you make to them. If you genuinely regard a person as important, it will show in subtle ways and establish a good foundation for effective communication.

3. **Look out for their interests.** "You can be the peachiest peach, but some people prefer oranges." I overheard a colleague say this once and it has stuck with me ever since. Try as you may, some people are never going to like you. They may envy you. You may belong to a group they have a difficult time getting along with. Or you may simply remind them of someone that hurt them in the past. Whether someone likes you or not, nothing prevents you from establishing a foundation of care and setting the stage for effective communication. Try looking out for their interest; not necessarily to build rapport but to improve communications. At a minimum, you'll convey that you're less interested in perpetuating a tense dynamic and more interested in building the type of dynamic required to deliver the outcomes you were both hired to deliver. In some cases, they will return the gesture. Over time, you may build an alliance that will pay dividends in terms of communication effectiveness.

Tailor

Thinking clarifies what you feel and what you intend to say, **listening** increases your chances of interpreting messages correctly and **caring** builds trust. If you do these things and then take steps to **tailor** your message, you'll significantly increase your chances of communicating effectively. Tailoring is about making your message easier to process. It's an essential step in remote work situations, where your listeners don't have as much nonverbal information as they would in face-to-face communication. To tailor your message, you must be salient, structured, and short.

Be Salient. The easiest messages to read are the ones your listeners want to read in the first place. Therefore, make your message salient by ensuring it meets a need. This goes back to intent. If your intent is to satisfy a need, then your reader will have an easier time reading it. Also, try to send messages your reader is interested in receiving. The best way to do this is to make sure that only pertinent stakeholders are on the distribution list. Further, always include an opt-out message like, "Please let me know if you'd like to be removed from this distribution list." The next thing you can do to increase saliency is, when possible, make sure your message is expected. If your audience is waiting on an update from you, they'll read it with interest. What each of these suggestions have in common is, they ensure you have a captive audience ahead of time. Finally, make sure your message is visually, audibly, and grammatically stimulating. You can achieve this by the way you structure the message, by selecting the best medium and by using an active voice. We'll cover structure and media selection later. Presently, we'll focus on using an active voice. An active voice is more salient than a passive voice. Instead of writing "Suggestions must be submitted by Thursday", write "Please submit your suggestions by Thursday." It's easier to read and it grabs the reader's attention by starting off with a word that suggests an action is coming. Your reader will be inclined to read on because they'll want to know what action you're requesting of them. Sentences in the active voice are shorter, clearer and more direct. They generally follow a simple structure of subject→verb→object. Keep your messages salient by using an active voice. Here are some additional examples.

PASSIVE VOICE	ACTIVE VOICE
Bananas are loved by monkeys.	Monkeys love bananas.
The cat was chased by the dog.	The dog chased the cat.
The money was counted by the man.	The man counted the money.

Be Structured. If you take time to structure your message, it will be more engaging and easier to read. To do this, think about the outcome your message is intended to produce. If you're proposing an idea, structure a Problem-Solution message. Clearly indicate both sections by using boldface, font size, capitalization, or a combination of these. If your intent is to help someone evaluate a solution, consider a Pros-Cons message structure. If you're submitting a set of options, use a bulleted list. Be sure to add visual hierarchy by bold facing a summary word at the start of each bulleted option. If you're sequencing a timeline of events, consider including a graphical element that summarizes the events in a visually pleasing manner. Any time investments you make along these lines will make your message more engaging. See **Appendix G** for examples of structured messages.

Be Short. Mark Twain wrote "I apologize for writing such a long letter, I didn't have time to write a short one." This clever play on words underscores that it takes considerably more time to write a short message than a long one. It's much easier to write *"I've asked all of the managers to submit a report that's easy to read and reflects the opinions of the entire group."* than it is to write *"The managers will work with their teams to simplify the report."* The longer sentence is 22 words. The shorter sentence is 11 words. To make this sentence half as long, I had to work on it twice as long. It's easy to understand why busy professionals will want to save time by sending overly verbose messages. To overcome this temptation, consider that verbose messages don't get read, they get skimmed. The following graphic is an eye scan report. It was generated by the Nielsen Norman Group[8], which conducted eye tracking research. The image was captured from a website that included several paragraphs of text. The intent of the study was to determine how much of the text would be read. It concluded that people scan webpages and phone screens in various patterns, one of them being in the shape of the letter F. One way to interpret these results is that readers will only read short messages that fall into an F pattern. Therefore, if you want your message to be read, keep it short.

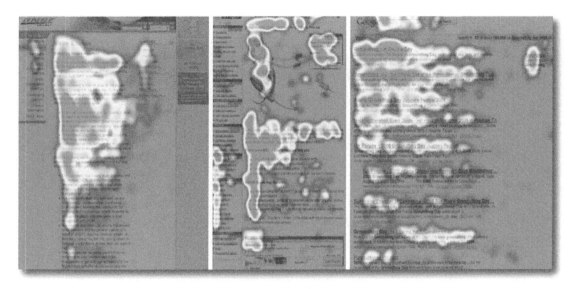

Source: http://www.nngroup.com/articles/f-shaped-pattern-reading-web-content/

Package

After you've done the hard work of thinking, listening, caring, and tailoring, you should think about how to package your message. Chefs understand this concept well. They not only focus on the taste of your meal, but how high it should sit on your plate, how the colors contrast and which dishes it should be served in. Similarly, you should consider how to package your message. The last thing you want to do is limit its impact by packaging it in an unworthy container. In communications, that container is your selection of medium. A medium (pl. media) is a device that moves messages over distance (E.g., smart phones) or through time (E.g., books) so that people who are not face to face can communicate. We'll narrow our focus to new media, which is digital or networked information and communication technologies.

The Ralphs Effect

The human dynamic changes based on communication medium. For example, we're far more courteous to one another at the grocery store, than we are on the freeway. I like to call this the **Ralphs effect**. Ralphs is my local grocery store. On the freeway, when we're going for the same lane, we cut one another off, beep at one another and have even been known to trade hand gestures. We lose this level of aggression at the grocery store—the **Ralphs effect**. When we're going for the same checkout lane at Ralphs, we're very courteous to one another.

Our exchanges often go like this:

- *"After you."*
- *"No. After you."*
- *"Go ahead. You don't have that many items any way."*
- *"Are you sure?"*
- *"Yes of course."*
- *"Thanks!"*
- *"Anytime!"*

Why are we more courteous at Ralphs than on the freeway? When I ask this question during webinars, the consensus is that when we're driving, our interactions are less personal. We dehumanize one another. But in Ralphs we're reminded of one another's humanity. Since this happens on the freeway, where we can see one another, it's no wonder it happens on the internet where our interactions are proxied by media. Your selection of media should factor in the Ralphs effect. Some interactions are best handled face to face or by phone, where each person's humanity is on full display. That said, to package your message in the worthiest container, you should expand your options, consider your goals, consider your recipient, and develop a communication plan. In addition to these considerations, you should publish a communication plan that clearly depicts how, when and to whom you will disseminate recurring communication updates.

Expand your Options

The first step in selecting your medium is to expand your options. Sending messages via email, text or even chat are quite common. To achieve uncommon communication effectiveness, you may need to make uncommon choices. There are ever expanding ways to package your message. Here's are 15 media options, most of which are generally overlooked.

Media Options		
Infographics	Message Boards	Blogs
Animated GIFS	In-house Social Media Platforms	Newsletters
Screensharing	Webinars	Videos
Whiteboards	Chat	Newsletters
Text	Phone	Email

By expanding your repertoire of communication mediums, you can communicate more powerfully and prolifically. I'm reminded of a communication proposal I submitted while managing projects at AT&T. My team was charged to virtualize several elements within the AT&T network. These were beachhead projects, meaning they had never been done before. As such, we were creating the template for a suite of projects that would follow. We already had a system in place for documenting processes, but it required users to read a lot of text and was rarely used. My communication proposal was to build a colorful web page that showed the process visually and allowed users to click on the parts of the process they were most interested in. After the proposal was approved, I partnered with a teammate and we built the page. The result? We got so many requests to access our page that we had to ask for additional storage capacity to handle the demand! By expanding our options, we were able to select a medium that resonated with our stakeholders and achieved our goal of sharing our knowledge across the organization. You can achieve similar results by expanding your media options. Once you do, the next step – consider your goals – will help you select the most effective medium.

Consider your Goals

What result are you trying to achieve with your message? What obstacles are you likely to face? Answering questions like these will help narrow your media choices. Do you expect there will be low interest in your message? Consider a more engaging medium like video. Do you need your audience to interact with your message? Consider a social media platform. Do you need to notify your reader of an event that's several weeks into the future? Consider Email. Do you need to resolve an issue? Consider a face-to-face interaction or a phone conversation. Do you need your communication in writing? Consider instant messaging or Email. Each communication medium can be effective in the right use case. The opposite is also true. Each medium can be ineffective in the wrong use case. For example, in the scenario I shared earlier, if we had used our pre-existing text-based process to share our knowledge of network virtualization projects, we would not have reached the right level of engagement. As a result, we would have been dragged into countless meetings to share what we had learned. You don't have to search hard to find examples of poor media selection choices. For example, Email is a poor medium for resolving a relationship problem. Animated GIFs can be a poor medium for formal communications but an excellent medium for training purposes. By considering your goals, you can select a medium that enhances your message and doesn't detract from it. The next step is to consider your recipient.

Consider your Recipient

Everyone has a preferred and a non-preferred communication medium. Some prefer texting. Others don't. Some hate voice mail messages. Others feel it's the clearest way to get their message across. Therefore, the first enhancement opportunity is clear. Communicate using your recipient's preferred medium – and not your own. If you're not sure what that is, just ask. Asking of course is the easy part. The difficult part is adjusting to their preferred style. If you do, your message will have a better chance of being read and interpreted correctly. The next consideration is whether they want to be a recipient in the first place. This is especially applicable to recipients on large distribution lists. You don't want to become that person who regularly sends unwanted mail to someone's already full inbox. You'll inadvertently train your receivers to ignore messages coming from you. The only way to avoid this is to comb through your distribution lists, person by person. If you're not sure who someone is, drop them a line through your chat system. Sending a note like the one below will be much appreciated and can lead to a great networking opportunity!

"Hi David. I noticed your name on my distribution list for Project X. Just wanted to confirm whether you find these updates helpful and still want to be included."

The final consideration is your relationship with the recipient. If the relationship is formal, sending a text message can make some recipients feel you're getting too personal too quickly - especially if there's a significant hierarchical gap between your position and theirs. If you have an informal relationship, consider the message you can send if you use a formal communication channel like email. You could inadvertently signal that you don't trust the recipient and would prefer to have the communication in writing. The point is, your selection of medium can send a message in itself. To enhance communication effectiveness, factor in the message of your medium. For example, the use of chat and text messages can imply trust and familiarity. Email messages can imply formality and the need for a paper trail, inferring a lack of trust. Some will interpret emoji's in Email messages as unprofessional. Others will appreciate your effort to limit misunderstanding. The important thing to bear in mind is that your message should cater to the whims, preferences, and idiosyncrasies of your recipient. This is the best way to ensure that the interpreted message matches your intended message.

Develop a Communication Plan

Expanding your communication options, and considering your goals and recipients will guide you in selecting the right medium for your message. Once you've done so, it's a good idea to determine which of your communication updates are ad hoc in nature and which are likely to recur. Recurring messages would include things like meeting minutes, weekly reports and regularly updated documents, like project schedules. One of the best ways to enhance communications in remote work scenarios is to publish a communication plan. A communication plan describes how, when and to whom recurring communications will be disseminated. It sets clear communication expectations for managers, teams and stakeholders. For example, if your stakeholders know that you send updated project schedules every Friday, they can relay that information to others without having to engage you. By publishing a communication plan for all recurring correspondence, you will increase communication efficiency and reinforce your sense of presence. To increase effectiveness, query your stakeholders and confirm how often they would like to receive updates. Be sure to include your boss in this process. Finally, post these updates in a location your stakeholders can easily reference. That way, if they opt out of receiving your notifications, they can find your latest updates on their own. See **Appendix H** for a customizable communication plan template.

Emotional Intelligence and Communication

Like performance, all emotional intelligence traits can positively impact communication. That said, the ones that are particularly meaningful in the context of communication in remote work situations are Emotional Self-Awareness, Emotional Expression and Stress Tolerance. Following are definitions of each emotional intelligence trait, indicators of high and low effectiveness and steps you can take to improve.

Emotional Self-Awareness

Since we've already discussed emotional self-awareness and its impact on communication at length in this chapter, we'll focus on definitions and indicators of high and low effectiveness. From an emotional intelligence standpoint, **emotional self-awareness** is the ability to recognize how you're feeling, why you're feeling that way and the impact your thoughts and feelings have on yourself and others. It includes the ability to differentiate between subtleties in emotions, like discerning between admiration, adoration, amusement, and romantic interest. The following table includes indicators of high and low effectiveness using this emotional intelligence trait.

Low Effectiveness	High Effectiveness
• Difficulty recognizing or identifying one's own emotions • Denies existence of emotions others can clearly see • Misreads and is misread by others	• Associates one's own feelings to appropriate causes • Able to differentiate between emotions • Reads people well and is read well by others

Follow the tactics prescribed earlier in the chapter to get better at emotional awareness. An additional step you can take to enhance your ability to discern between subtleties in emotions, is to look up the definitions of the 60 emotions provided earlier in the "Expand Your Emotional Vocabulary" section.

Emotional Expression

Emotional expression is about controlling how you come across to others and congruency between your verbal and nonverbal messages. Even when we're not speaking, we send out messages at an emotional level. Emotional expression is about being aware of those messages and taking effective steps to control them. From an emotional intelligence standpoint, **emotional expression** is the open and deliberate expression of verbal and nonverbal messages. The following table includes indicators of high and low effectiveness using this emotional intelligence trait.

Low Effectiveness	High Effectiveness
• Appears withdrawn • Difficult to read • Comes across in a way that is inconsistent with how one feels	• Expresses themselves easily • Often described by others as "real" • Easy to read

As mentioned earlier, the best way to control the non-verbal messages you send is to be sincere. This will increase verbal and non-verbal congruency. It's also helpful to be more deliberate with your body language, timing language and tonal language. To be even more effective, take a few tips from professionals who have mastered the art of coming across exactly as they intend to—actors and actresses. Thespians take full control of their non-verbal and verbal messages to convey the precise message their aiming for. Here are a few of their guidelines.

1. **Take an acting class.** This may come as a surprise to some, but there are very few instant actors. According to Janine Hawley, Associate Professor of Voice in the School of Drama and director of Acting Out!, "It generally takes a great deal of time and practice to hone one's skills." Naturally, an acting class will include things that are only relevant to those pursuing an acting career, but it also includes training you can't find anywhere else, like developing physicality, physical gesturing, dialect coaching, improvisation, and active empathy. Some of these classes are offered OnDemand for less than one might expect. You can also get excellent tips for free on YouTube. The usefulness of learning skills that are complimentary to your profession was validated by the late NFL running back Walter Payton, who is regarded as one of the greatest American football players of all time. Payton studied ballet while playing football for the Chicago Bears. Ballet dancers are considered by many to be the best athletes in the world; a fact that led some to conclude that this may have been the secret to his success.

2. **Know what your character (you) wants.** This tactic expands on the idea that sincerity triggers non-verbal cues that naturally support the messages you convey. Thespians use the knowledge of what their character wants to advise their delivery of verbal and nonverbal messages. For example, they may ask themselves "how would my character respond to this, given what they want from this exchange?" Similar, by keeping your long-term and short-term objectives in view, you can rely on your natural instinct to send non-verbal cues that support the message you're intending to convey.

3. **Film yourself.** The best course I've taken on public speaking was one where the instructor filmed each participant giving a presentation in the morning and had the entire class critique us in the afternoon. She paused each person's video at some of their most unflattering moments. It was a grueling session and everyone was eager to get their critique over with. When my turn came, I was especially impacted by how wildly I flailed my arms when I wanted to emphasize a point. My gestures were so animated that they distracted from my message and made me appear giddy. Also, I had what looked like a smirk on my face when I was confident what I was going to say next. This made me

appear overconfident and at times, condescending. Finally, when I made a point about which I was passionate, my face looked almost angry. Although I felt none of those emotions during my presentation, that is how I came across to myself and others who watched the video. Since taking that course, I've continued the practice of filming myself from time to time to check my verbal and non-verbal congruency. I don't use prepared presentations when I do this. I use real messages I intend to convey that week. This has helped immensely in controlling the inadvertent messages I send. As I mentioned earlier, sincerity is an excellent starting point, but this alone will not guarantee non-verbal congruency. By filming yourself, you can catch and correct small quirks that detract from your message. For example, I have discovered that I can always stand to smile more. It helps me to come across more confident and helpful and less forceful and preachy.

Stress Tolerance

No one has ever responded to any message you've ever conveyed. They have always responded to their interpretation of the messages you've conveyed. This is the reason we've dedicated so much focus to the interpreted message. The better you can control your messages the greater the likelihood that your listeners will react to the messages you intended and not their misinterpretations of them. Notwithstanding, despite your best efforts, communication disconnects are certain to occur in remote work situations. As mentioned earlier, new media can hinder our ability to correctly interpret messages by removing up to 93% of the information we need to do so. Moreover, communication disconnects can become explosive when either party feels disrespected or doubts the other's intentions. Therefore, it's important to develop effective coping mechanisms and a robust tolerance for difficult and stressful communication exchanges. This is where stress tolerance can help. From an emotional intelligence standpoint, **stress tolerance** is the ability to cope with stressful or difficult situations and a firm belief that you can manage or influence the situation in a positive manner. It involves the capacity to choose an effective course of action to withstand and address adverse events and stressful situations. The following table includes indicators of high and low effectiveness using this emotional intelligence trait.

Low Effectiveness	High Effectiveness
• Poor or non-existent coping strategies • Reactive • Avoids conflict or gives in too easily	• Maintains influence and control • Effective coping strategies • Graceful under fire

The key to increasing stress tolerance is to increase the quantity and quality of your coping tactics. The better prepared you are for difficult communication exchanges, the more confident and calm you will be throughout them and the more effectively you will resolve them. If you have a limited supply of tactics, a good reference is *Crucial Conversations*[9], by Patterson, Grenny, McMillan and Switzler. Following are some of my go-to tactics, honed from this and other resources.

1. **Prioritize Safety.** Safety is the condition of being protected from harm or other undesirable outcomes. When communicating, conditions are "safe" when your listener feels respected and trusts your intentions. When a listener feels disrespected by you or has interpreted your intentions toward them as harmful, safety has been compromised. When this occurs, it's futile to continue. Prioritizing safety is about training yourself to recognize when safety has been compromised and suspending your discourse until it has been restored. By putting safety first, you will create an environment that is conducive for conflict resolution.

2. **Learn to Identify Unsafe Conditions.** To disrupt unhealthy communication exchanges, you must be able to detect when safety has been compromised. The book *Crucial Conversations* offers the following six indicators that safety has been compromised.

   • **Masking** – When either party begins to understate their true opinions by using sarcasm or "sugarcoating" the truth. **Example**: "No, I don't mind that you left me off the report. I love being unrecognized!"

   • **Avoiding** – When either party continues the exchange but avoids a sensitive topic. Example: "Yea, I got your message, but I've been busy, and we should probably use this meeting to develop the timeline".

- **Withdrawing** – When either party exits the exchange altogether. Example: "I'd love to get into this, but something came up and I must end our meeting early today".

- **Controlling** - When either party begins to dominate the exchange by overstating facts, cutting the other person off, or bombarding them with questions. Example: "We've tried them before, and it was a total disaster! Everyone knows they have the worst customer service on the planet!"

- **Labeling** - When either party uses a label to categorically dismiss people or ideas, usually under a general stereotype. Example: "Why listen to her? She's from corporate. Need I say more?"

- **Attacking** - When either party makes the other party suffer by belittling them, shouting at them, or threatening them. Example: "I don't mean to shout, but it seems like my team always ends up holding the bag."

When you spot these conditions, suspend your discourse and work with your listener to restore psychological safety.

3. **Restore Safety.** Restoring safety is a simple tactic to understand and a difficult one to master. Recall that one of the main causes of ineffective communication exchanges is when your listener has not perceived the proper level of respect from you or has interpreted your intentions toward them as harmful. Therefore, to restore safety you'll need to clarify what you **are not** trying to do and what you **are** trying to do. What makes this simple process difficult to master is that when you need to use it, you may be emotionally jarred yourself. The following four-step process was adopted from tactics included in the book *Crucial Conversations*.

- **Clarify** that you **are not** disrespectful of them.

- **Clarify** that you **are not** trying to harm them.

- **Clarify** that you **are** respectful of them.

- **Clarify** that you **are** trying to achieve a constructive purpose.

Following are two scenarios depicting this four-step process.

SCENARIO 1:

A co-worker suspects a peer of overshadowing their work.

- Clarify that you **are not** disrespectful of them.

Example: *"The last thing I wanted to do was communicate that I don't value the work you put in."*

- Clarify that you **are not** trying to harm them.

Example: *"My intention is not to highlight my portion of the work over yours."*

- Clarify that you **are** respectful of them.

Example: *"I respect and value your contributions."*

- Clarify that you **are** trying to achieve a constructive purpose.

Example: *"My goal is to present our combined work in a logical sequence, irrespective of whose work appears first."*

SCENARIO 2

An employee feels their manager doesn't trust them to deliver a project.

- Clarify that you **are not** disrespectful of them.

Example: *"I don't mean to imply that I don't think you can manage this project."*

- Clarify that you **are not** trying to harm them.

Example: *"I don't mean to undermine your decisions."*

- Clarify that you **are** respectful of them.

Example: *"I respect the way you manage your projects."*

- Clarify that you **are** trying to achieve a constructive purpose.

Example: *"I've decided to reallocate resources across the team to better align with the new strategic initiatives."*

The key to making this process work is to do each step, despite how repetitive it may seem. When conflict occurs, emotions can be high. Taking a slow, repetitive, deliberate approach will improve the chances of your message getting through.

Chapter Summary

In this chapter we addressed "the single biggest problem in communication", which is the illusion that it has taken place. We proposed strategies to turn the illusion of effective communication into reality by simplifying messages to increase the likelihood that the interpreted message will match your intended message. To simply messages, we presented tactics around thinking through thoughts and intentions, listening to non-verbal cues, caring for your recipient, tailoring your message, and packaging it in the most effective medium. We concluded with strategies for increasing emotional intelligence in the areas of Emotional Self-Awareness, Emotional Expression and Stress Tolerance. For one additional tactic, see **Appendix E** which includes guidance for facilitating result-oriented meetings versus non-result-oriented meetings. Result-oriented meetings deliver valid, tangible results. They are shorter than non-result-oriented meetings and are included in **Appendix C** as a tactic for battling Zoom Fatigue. Communication can be effective across any medium. The further technology moves us from face-to-face communications, the harder we must work to ensure the messages we send are interpreted as we intended.

References

1. Mehrabian, Albert. Silent Messages. Wadsworth, 1971.

2. Selye, Hans. Stress without Distress. Signet, 1974.

3. Radhakrishnan, Rohini. "What Are the 27 Basic Emotions" medicinenet.com, MedicineNet, 12/1/20, https://www.medicinenet.com/what_are_the_27_basic_emotions/article.htm

4. Zinsser, William. On Writing Well. HarperCollins, 2006.

5. Hargie, Owen. Skilled Interpersonal Communication. Routledge. 2017

6. Gesteland, Richard. Cross-Cultural Business Behavior. Copenhagen Business School Press. 2012

7. Jones, Richard. Communication in the Real World. Flatworld. 2017

8. Pernice, Kara. "F-Shaped Pattern of Reading on the Web: Misunderstood, But Still Relevant (Even on Mobile)" nngroup.com, Nielson Norman Group, 11/12/17, https://www.nngroup.com/articles/f-shaped-pattern-reading-web-content/

9. Patterson, Grenny, McMillan and Switzler. Crucial Conversations. McGraw-Hill Education, 2011.

Conclusion

Zoom Fatigue. The Work from Home Economy. Social Distancing. These terms were not in circulation at the start of 2020. They emerged abruptly, alongside our hastily launched mobile workforces. Would that the world of business had advanced notice of the pandemic crisis. We would have used the time to ensure our workforces were truly ready, and not just from a technical standpoint. We would have trained our professionals to establish a sense of presence, both as workers and leaders. We would have trained them to deliver optimal performance from any location and to inspire optimal performance by balancing trust with accountability. We would have encouraged them to evaluate their predisposition to extend trust and trained them to earn trust and close trust gaps. We would have also trained them to effectively communicate from remote locations. Notwithstanding, the most effective professionals and leaders will do these things now and continue to close gaps in **REMOTEtional Intelligence**. This isn't the first time something as important as a mobile workforce was hastily launched. Most initiatives launched in response to a crisis don't have the luxury of careful planning. What differentiates crisis-response initiatives that are sustainable from those that aren't is the degree to which we go back and close the process and skill gaps afterwards. Now is as good a time as any to do the things we would have done if we had the benefit of advanced warning.

APPENDICES

Appendix A
Seven Common Concerns about Remote Work

Despite the promise of remote work, some have concerns that will not be dissipated by studies and statistics. Following are seven common concerns about remote work and responses that can be used as a starting point for addressing management and employee concerns about working remotely.

7 Concerns About Remote Work
Concern #1
I'm note sure I like working alone.
Response
Working alone is not an entirely new dynamic. Even in the office, a lot of communication happens <u>remotely</u>, via phone, e-mail, chat or conference calls. The chief difference is, you won't be interrupted by people stopping by your desk to chat or ask questions.
Working remotely, you can have all the contact time you want and more of the quiet time you need to focus on a tasks.
Concern #2
Once my team starts working remotely, I'll never see or hear from them again.
Response
Create an environment where your direct reports not only feel comfortable contacting you, but they want to. Resist the urge to check in under false pretenses, as this erodes trust and credibility. Instead, schedule recurring 1-on-1 meetings and be sure to keep them. Be easy to reach and let your team know when you'll be free each day. When managing remote workers, contact them more often to offer praise or useful information than critique, so they look forward to hearing from you. A 3:1 ratio of praise to critique is a good target. See Chapter 2 (Presence) and Chapter 4 (Trust) for relevant strategies.

7 Concerns About Remote Work

Concern #3

Worker productivity will drop because I'm not able to monitor my employees as well as I can in the office.

Response

According to a study published by SHRM in 2015, most organizations that encourage remote work experience productivity improvements, and no decline in job performance attributable to working remotely. Remote workers log an average of 7 more hours per week and are more productive even when they're sick. In most cases, you'll see improvements in productivity and quality. If you experience the opposite from an employee who previously was a solid performer, start by investigating whether they're experiencing a remote worker readiness issue. See Chapter 1 (Readiness), and Chapter3 (Performance) for relevant strategies.

Concern #4

Will I be able to separate home and work?

Response

Physically, you must identify where you can have the equipment and the working environment you need. Ensure there's enough room to do your work. Collaborate with your household about noise levels, especially during conference calls. Post your meeting schedule each day so they know when to be super quiet. Let them know when you must focus exclusively on work and when your breaks are, so you can focus on them. Make it fun. Make your breaks a shared experience. Plan special outings, even if it's just lunch on the patio. See Chapter 1 (Readiness) for relevant strategies.

7 Concerns About Remote Work

Concern #5

Remote work prevents effective collaboration.

Response

Effective collaboration is more attributable to team synergy than collaborative workspaces. Effective work planning and communication strategies can support teams across varying time zones and geographies. Functional teams collaborate to establish their own procedures for working together. Typically, these will include a mix of one-off meetings, ad hoc phone conversations, conference calls, email, and instant messaging—none of which are disrupted by remote work. Conversely, teams that were dysfunctional prior to the pandemic will experience significant challenges. See Chapter 5 (Communication) for relevant strategies. Also, consider taking the course "Transcend Team Dysfunction", offered on pmplicity.com.

Concern #6

I'm not sure I can I live up to my manager's expectations from a remote location.

Response

The best way to meet your manger's expectations is to create reasonable ones together and commit to meeting them. Communication is the key. Jointly define what's reasonable for your availability, productivity, and response times. Develop a clear communication plan. Ideally, your manager will proactively express concerns as they come up. Bear in mind that concerns can be difficult to clarify due to poor performance imposters like the ones covered in Chapter 1. If you sense something in the air, be more curious than defensive and work together to bring it to the surface. Be mindful that remote work will expose trust gaps on either side. You'll need a clear strategy for proactively closing trust gaps. See Chapter 3 (Performance) and Chapter 4 (Trust) for relevant strategies.

7 Concerns About Remote Work

Concern #7

Remote work might jeopardize my chances for advancement.

Response

This is a valid concern. In theory, advancement shouldn't be impacted by where one completes the work. In reality, a manager's perception of your performance is the decisive factor when it comes to advancement. You can help yourself and your manager by maintaining a high level of communication. Provide regular updates on your work. Keep track of your accomplishments and review them with your manager during 1-on-1 meetings. Be sure to share positive feedback from customers, colleagues and stakeholders. Sometimes you may want to solicit such feedback and ask for it in writing. When working remotely, it's in your best interest to provide specific, verifiable, evidence of your performance. See Chapter 2 (Presence) and Chapter 3 (Performance) for relevant strategies.

Appendix B

Background and Video Specs by Platform

Zoom Specs

<u>Custom Background Images</u>

Zoom has no virtual background image size restrictions but recommends you crop your image to match the aspect ratio of your camera before uploading one to their platform. If your camera is set to 16:9, an image that is 1280 by 720 pixels or 1920 by 1080 pixels would work well.

<u>Custom Background Videos</u>

For video backgrounds, Zoom recommends mp4 or mov files with a minimum resolution of 480 by 360 pixels (360p) and a maximum resolution of 1280 by 720 (720p) pixels.

Webex Specs

<u>Custom and Blurred Background Images</u>

Webex allows users to blur their backgrounds. Here are the steps.

1. Click Blur

2. To use a default virtual background, click the one you want.

3. To use your own image for the virtual background, tap the + icon.

<u>Custom Background Images</u>

WebEx recommends that you use an image that's 1280 × 720 pixels in size or larger. Images must be in the .jpg or .png format.

<u>Custom Background Videos</u>

As of the time of this publication, supported virtual background file formats include: BMP, GIF, JPEG, PNG. Animated GIFs aren't supported. Popular video file types, such as .mov and .mpg are not included.

Skype Specs

Custom and Blurred Background Images

Skype also allows users to blur their backgrounds. Here are the steps.

1. Hover over the **video** button or click the ⋯ **More** menu.

2. Click **Choose background effect**.

3. You can **Blur** the room you're in currently, choose one of the predefined images or an image you previously added, or **Add** a new **image** to customize your background effect. To see all the predefined image categories, select the ⋯ **More** icon under **Choose background effect**.

Skype recommends using images in landscape orientation. Also, the custom image must be saved locally on your desktop.

Custom Background Videos

We were unable to locate instructions for uploading custom background videos to Skype. This option is likely not available as of the time of this publication.

Google Meet Specs

Custom and Blurred Background Images

Google Meet also allows users to blur their backgrounds. Here are the steps.

1. Go to **Google Meet** ➤select a meeting.

2. On the bottom right of your self view, click **Change Background**.

   ▪ To completely blur your background, click **Blur** your background .

   ▪ To slightly blur your background, click **Slightly blur** your background .

   ▪ To select a pre-uploaded background, click a background.

   ▪ To upload your own image for your background, click **Add +**.

3. Click **Join Now**.

Custom Background Videos

We were unable to locate instructions for uploading custom background videos to Google Meet. This option is likely not available as of the time of this publication.

Appendix C – Battling "Zoom Fatigue" – 10 Tips

Zoom fatigue is caused by several things, including:

- Staring directly into the camera for extended periods of time

- Undivided, uninterrupted focus on one subject

- Sitting for extended periods of time without standing up or walking around

- Back-to-back meetings

- Ineffectively run meetings

Here are ten tips for battling Zoom Fatigue:

1. **Run result-oriented meetings.** If you're a meeting organizer, challenge yourself to identify the specific result(s) your meeting should produce. If you can't, consider canceling it. We've provided a list of valid results that warrant a meeting and guidelines for running shorter meetings in **Appendix E** (Result-Oriented Meetings).

2. **Add a time buffer between calls.** Few things are more tiring than back-to-back video meetings. If you're a meeting organizer, always make it a point to end your meeting early (ideally 20 minutes early). Your attendees will thank you profusely and you will afford yourself a much-needed breather. If you're not the meeting organizer, monitor your schedule often and consider adding a buffer immediately after a meeting gets scheduled onto your calendar. Make sure others can see your buffer so they don't schedule over it.

3. **Turn your camera off from time to time.** Take a professional headshot and post it in place of your video when you want to take a quick stretch break, eat a quick snack, or walk around for a second. The professional headshot will keep keep you looking professional and engaged while you take a stretch break.

4. **Make your meeting optional.** Optional meetings can have the opposite effect from what you might think. By making it optional, you will guarantee a captive audience. Everyone there will have chosen to be there. This will ensure more engagement and less Zoom fatigue. If you're discussing something important, record the meeting so others can listen when their schedule allows.

5. **Switch the medium.** If you get Zoom Fatigue by 2PM, consider switching the medium for your remaining meetings. Chances are, if you're experiencing Zoom Fatigue, so are others. Consider opening a chat room, having a phone conversation, or sending an email in place of your meeting.

6. **Have a voice-only meeting.** We've all been doing conference calls for years. Why is Zoom fatigue only occurring now? This is because over time, we've shifted from video-optional meetings to video-expected meetings. When you turn the cameras off, you can stand up, eat your snack, or even step away for a short while without appearing rude or disengaged. Consider mixing things up a bit by having a few voice-only meetings.

7. **Multitask.** How many times per week do you attend 60-minute meetings where your area of concern is only discussed for 5 minutes? If your answer is greater than three, you have identified some of your Zoom Fatigue culprits. Make better use of those 55-minute intervals. Consider selective multitasking. Alert the meeting organizer ahead of time that you will be attending their meeting audio-only. Then, identify tasks that don't require much focus, like formatting a report or processing a form, and chip away at them until it's your turn to speak.

8. **Opt-out.** Sometimes your action item is required, but not your attendance. I'm reminded of an engineer I worked with at AT&T who would send me his updates the morning of my weekly project meetings. He would end his update by asking "do you still need me on the call?" My answer was always "No." He had figured out that what I really needed from him was his action item and not his attendance.

9. **Schedule Meeting Days and Non-Meeting Days.** If you're a meeting organizer, schedule the bulk of your meetings across two or three days. This will allow you to make time for administrative tasks or tasks that require focused time. It will also limit Zoom fatigue by allow you to prepare yourself in advance and schedule in buffers between your meetings. If you're not the meeting organizer, you can do the same thing by letting meeting organizers know that your preferred meeting times are on the days you've determined to be your meeting days.

10. **Comment on something funny or amusing.** If you're experiencing Zoom Fatigue, there's a good chance someone else is too. Try lightening the mood by commenting on something funny or amusing at the start of a meeting. If it gets a laugh or if others join in on the fun, this can be a welcome distraction and make the meeting more interesting. The more Zoom Fatigue there is, the more people will want to keep it going. If you're the meeting organizer, make room for this diversion and reference it at some point during the meeting. Sometimes a small amount of levity can create the mental stretch break needed for a productive meeting.

Appendix D – Going Back into the Office – 12 Things to Expect

1. **Emotional Reactions** – Workers may have a range of emotional reactions toward returning to the office. Some will welcome the opportunity to get back to socializing with coworkers and compartmentalizing their lives again between home and work. Others may feel anxiety due to fear of getting sick or resentment due to feeling pressured to return when they're not ready or due to having to take a vaccine they may not otherwise be inclined to take.

2. **Distanced seating** – Expect social distancing to continue in the form of distanced seating.

3. **Fewer seats** – Some businesses will apply lessons learned from restaurateurs and remove some seats and cubicles as a means of ensuring social distancing.

4. **Phased returns** – Not everyone will return at once. Many will implement phased returns to get employee feedback, apply lessons learned and establish best practices.

5. **Essential worker designations** – As with other work stoppage events, some positions will be deemed essential to establish phased return priorities and to identify work that can be best performed in the office.

6. **More designated seating** – To limit the spread of the virus, some employers may encourage designated seating.

7. **Possible shift work** – Distanced seating requirements will create space constraints that some employer may resolve through shift work.

8. **Isolation Rooms** – Some employers may designate isolation rooms for employees that develop symptoms throughout the workday.

9. **Pre-screening** – Most employers will implement a screening protocol to deem an employee safe to return to the office.

10. **Cleaning during Business hours** – Cleaning will no longer be designated to after-work hours. Many employers will implement cleaning protocols during the day to not only maintain clean environments but also for the psychological reassurance of workers that the work environment is safe.

11. **Flexible Work Policies** – Many employers will implement work-from-home policies where employees can work routinely from home several days per week.

12. **Fits and Starts** – Employers will likely adjust return-to-work policies quite fluidly as new learnings unfold. As such, there are likely to be several "fits and starts" before long-term policies emerge.

Appendix E – Result-Oriented Meetings

Dave Barry said *"If you had to identify, in a word, the reason why the human race has not achieved, and never will achieve its full potential, that word would be 'meetings'."* His sentiments are shared by many working professionals whose precious hours are wasted in non-result-oriented meetings. Non-result-oriented meeting will generally last the entire allotted time — not because there are 60 minutes' worth of actionable work — but because 60 minutes is how long the meeting was scheduled for. Participants may discuss the project for which the meeting was scheduled, but progress will be much slower than it could be and the meeting will last much longer than it should. Conversely, result-oriented meetings are scheduled to deliver valid, tangible results. Following are ten meeting outcomes that constitute valid reasons to meet. If your meeting will not produce similar outcomes, consider postponing it until you can clearly identify the results you want your meeting to produce.

1. We are meeting to confirm we have 100% of the resources we need to start our project.

2. We are meeting to assign roles and responsibilities.

3. We are meeting to decompose our project into manageable parts and divide the work amongst our team.

4. We are meeting to get time estimates from each team member and ultimately develop a project schedule.

5. We are meeting to get cost estimates from each team member and ultimately develop a project budget.

6. We are meeting to make a Go or No-Go decision.

7. We are meeting to get everyone's feedback on a proposal or initiative.

8. We are meeting to establish performance targets for the upcoming year.

9. We are meeting to prioritize our strategic initiatives.

10. We are meeting to brainstorm ideas for an upcoming event or initiative.

Naturally, every meeting or meeting series will not meet criteria like these. For example, some meetings may be scheduled to build team synergy or keep team members current on business direction. Notwithstanding, meetings such as weekly team or operational meetings should be re-visited periodically to confirm they are delivering the results for which they were scheduled and that the format is ideal for accomplishing those results.

Finally, if you're hosting recurring project meetings versus recurring operational meetings, you should have an idea what results you should have delivered after so many meetings. For example, if you plan to develop a draft project schedule or budget within the first four project meetings, you can structure your agenda to drive toward those results. Your project team will detect your sense of purpose and this will make them more engaged as active meeting participants. Any effort you make toward running result-oriented meetings will decrease Zoom Fatigue and allow you to deliver more results in less time. In my experience, result oriented meetings are shorter and more productive than non-result-oriented meetings. This is because it rarely takes a full hour to deliver hard results. Also, when you're clear what results you're after, you can confidently and credibly end your meetings early once you've achieved them.

Appendix F – The EQi 2.0 Model

EQi 2.0 is an emotional intelligence assessment that can be taken online. It includes 133 questions and must be administered by an EQi 2.0–certified practitioner. Unlike other Emotional Intelligence Assessments, the EQi 2.0 is a Level B instrument, which means it satisfies the following requirements:

- **Reliability** – Its results are consistent and reproducible.

- **Validity** – It measures what it's designed to measure.

- **Normed** – Involved at least 500 sample participants and is representative of participants from varying gender and age groups.

- **Researched** – Results are related to real outcomes and based on a theoretical model.

- **Supporting Material** – It is supported by documented theory, research and training and development resources.

- **Subject Expertise** – Its authors and developers have the requisite credentials and experience and their results have been peer reviewed.

Participants who complete the EQi 2.0 assessment will receive a comprehensive report, which will include their emotional intelligence score, how they scored in each of the five composite areas and each of the 15 subscales, and how their results compare with statistical norms.

The five composite areas and the 15 subscales measured by the EQi 2.0 instrument are listed below.

Self-Perception	Self-Expression	Interpersonal Skills	Desicion Making Skills	Stress Management Skills
Self-Regard	Emotional Expression	Interpersonal Relationships	Problem Solving	Flexibility
Self-Actualization	Assertiveness	Empathy	Reality Testing	Stress Tolerance
Emotional Self-Awareness	Independence	Social Responsibility	Impulse Control	Optimism

About Your Emotional Intelligence Score

About 50% of the general population has an emotional intelligence score of between 90 and 110, with the average score being 100. About 25% of the general population scores below 90 and about 25% score above 110, which is considered the high emotional intelligence range.

Despite these typical outcomes, there is no such thing as a "bad" emotional intelligence score. The goal of taking an emotional intelligence assessment is not to get a high score, but rather to gain insights for becoming more effective at perceiving yourself, expressing yourself, developing and maintaining social relationships, coping with challenges, and using emotional information. A high emotional intelligence score is far less useful than a clear understanding of where you can improve to become more effective.

How to take the EQi 2.0 Emotional Intelligence Assessment

If you would like to take the EQi 2.0 assessment and learn where you should concentrate your efforts to become more effective, scan the QR code below or visit **https://calendly.com/pmplicity/15min** to schedule a free 15-minute consultation. During your consultation, be sure to mention that you purchased this book to receive $50.00 off the $300.00 assessment fee.

Appendix G – Examples of Structured Messages

Example 1 – Problem Solution Message

Hi Sue,

Here's a quick recap of the problem we discussed earlier and three possible solutions. Let me know what you think.

Problem

Deforestation is a serious problem because trees clean the air, store water, preserve soil and provide homes for animals. They also meet human needs including supplying food, fuel and wood products like paper.

Solution 1

Implement a policy to use both sides of the paper when photocopying.

Solution 2

Encourage maximum utilization of paper products, like using the same Styrofoam cup throughout the day.

Solution 3

Launch a paper recycling program.

Example 2 – Pros/Cons Message

Hi Ali,

I've queried the team about their thoughts on migrating from the Windows to the Linux operating system. I've summarized their feedback in the following Pros and Cons statements. Let me know if I can assist further.

Pros

- Cost savings
- Exploit latest available features
- Match our competitor's speed
- Access to the source code

Cons

- Security concerns due to open source

- Stability concerns

- Loss of Microsoft Support agreement

- End user lockdown issues

Appendix H – Communication Plan Template

Description	Audience	Frequency	Delivery Media
Project Meetings	• Project Team • Project Sponsor	Weekly	• Video Conference
Project Status Report	• Executive Team • Manager • Project Sponsor • Project Team	Weekly	• Email • Team Page
Program Status Report	• Executive Team • Manager • Project Sponsor	Monthlty	• Email • Team Page
Meeting Minutes	• Meeting Attendees	Within 48 hours	• Email • Team Page
Issue Tracker	• Project Team • Project Sponsor • Manager	Weekly	• Email • Team Page
Risk Tracker	• Project Team • Project Sponsor • Manager	Monthly	• Email • Team Page
Cost Tracker	• Executive Team • Manager • Project Sponsor • Project Team	Quarterly	• Email • Team Page
Project Schedule	• Project Team • Project Sponsor	Weekly	• Email • Team Page

Index

Jerry Reed, PMP, CSM, MCP, EQi

Jerry Reed is an award-winning instructor, speaker, author, and project management consultant. He has delivered lectures, workshops, seminars and webinars to managers and technology workers from Google, AT&T, PMI, Optum Rx, UCLA, SpaceX, the United Nations, Blizzard, Disney, Netflix and other organizations. His original, content-rich, high-energy programs are well-researched and presented in a professional and engaging style.

With over 20 years of project management experience, Jerry has successfully delivered over 100 projects as a senior project manager with AT&T, an engineer with NI-Gas and a research engineer with the US Army Corp. of Engineers. Mr. Reed has a Bachelor of Science degree in Mechanical Engineering from the University of Illinois, at Urbana-Champaign. He is PMP-certified, a Microsoft-Certified Professional, a certified emotional intelligence practitioner and a marathon runner. Jerry has taught project leadership and scheduling courses for over 10 years at UCLA Extension and was awarded UCLA Distinguished Instructor in 2014. He has served on the UCLA Extension Project Management Advisory Board, co-founded PMplicity, and authored Microsoft Project 2019 B.A.S.I.C.S.

Yolanda Reed, CSM

Yolanda Reed is an author, editor, Certified Scrum Master, seasoned administrator, graphic artist and certified fitness professional. As Principal Administrator, she manages daily operations, office communications, client billing, vendor correspondence and accounting. She performs a wide variety of project management, product development, quality assurance and administrative functions. She prepares meeting material, conducts research for proposals, prepares status reports and compiles data to educate and provide recommendations.Yolanda is the "secret sauce" of PMplicity. She maintains strong client relationships and is the primary liaison for PMPlicity partners, including Amazon, Apple, Vimeo, Barnes and Noble and UCLA.

Live Training Events

REMOTEtional Intelligence is part of a 5-part live training series, available though pmplicity.com. Other live training events include:

- Make it Manageable

- Transcending Team Dysfunction

- Adapt and Win!

- 30 Days Faster!

To register for the next REMOTEtional Intelligence live training event, visit **https://www.pmplicity.com/play1** or scan the QR code below.

Made in the USA
Coppell, TX
14 January 2022

71597906R00109